"Esther's heart for Ukrainian people and her love of sharing inspirational stories blend perfectly in *Hope for Ukraine*, reminding us that even in the darkest times, there is light."

Mark Batterson, *New York Times* bestselling author

"As the war in Ukraine continues, stories of heroism, bravery, and tragedy are emerging every day. In this book you will meet normal people whose lives have been turned upside down by events outside of their control. Yet in the midst of it all, God is still at work. In the midst of the pain, there is hope."

Dr. Michael Brown, host, *Line of Fire* radio broadcast;
author, *Has God Failed You?*

"A heartrending yet inspiring collection of stories from the front line of this great and tragic conflict. A fuel for prayer and political engagement."

Pete Greig, 24-7 Prayer International

D1372728

HOPE
FOR
UKRAINE

HOPE

FOR
UKRAINE

STORIES OF GRIT AND GRACE
FROM THE FRONT LINES OF WAR

KYLE DUNCAN AND ESTHER FEDORKEVICH

Chosen

a division of Baker Publishing Group
Minneapolis, Minnesota

© 2022 by Kyle Duncan and Esther Fedorkevich

Published by Chosen Books
Minneapolis, Minnesota
www.chosenbooks.com

Chosen Books is a division of
Baker Publishing Group, Grand Rapids, Michigan

Printed in the United States of America

ISBN 978-0-8007-6323-7 (trade paper)
ISBN 978-1-4934-4105-1 (ebook)
ISBN 978-0-8007-6344-2 (casebound)

Library of Congress Cataloging-in-Publication Control Number: 2022028322

Scripture quotations are from THE HOLY BIBLE, NEW INTERNATIONAL VERSION®, NIV© Copyright © 1973, 1978, 1984 by Biblica, Inc.® Used by permission. All rights reserved worldwide.

Cover design by Rob Williams, InsideOut Creative Arts, Inc.

Authors represented by The Fedd Agency, Inc.

Baker Publishing Group publications use paper produced from sustainable forestry practices and post-consumer waste whenever possible.

22   23   24   25   26   27   28   7   6   5   4   3   2   1

To Cory "Jhenya" Duncan, who inspired all this
—Kyle

To my Ukrainian grandparents
—Esther

Contents

Contents

Foreword

We love the people of Ukraine and have both had the privilege of ministering in their nation. What stood out to us most was their unrelenting resilience, genuine kindness, and gracious generosity. I can still remember a very special lunch. Our family was hosted in the home of a Ukrainian mother and her three daughters. They were Christians who had immigrated to the United States. After lunch we sat in their living room as the daughters played Vivaldi with such passion and excellence that we wept.

What we experienced that day typifies the tenacious Ukrainian beauty. It is a nation that has endured the cruelty of both communism and war, yet its people cling to the belief that they are destined for more. Our hearts sank when we heard the news of the Russian invasion, and like so many, our team is praying for a swift resolution so that justice and peace would again reign in their land.

When we heard Kyle Duncan and Esther Fedorkevich had compiled a book to grant each of us a window into the lives of these extraordinary people, we were honored to add our voice to theirs. As you read, let's believe in the hope that one day the destiny of Ukraine will far surpass the pain of her history.

John and Lisa Bevere, co-founders, Messenger International;
bestselling authors and ministers

Acknowledgments

K yle would like to thank . . .

My wife, Suzanne—here's to my best friend and partner, who has loved me in the worst of times and the best. My daughters, Hannah, Kylie, and Zoe, for helping me laugh in the midst of chaos. My son, Cory "Jhenya," for showing me the face of bravery—your Ukrainian heart is huge.

My siblings Kimmy, Kirk, and Krissy, for your unconditional support. My sister Kerry—our sunset beach walks provided the fuel for my often-empty tank. My mom, Stella Frances Duncan—those childhood trips to the Glendale Public Library paid off, Mom. And my late dad, Robert, who modeled a love for both God and the arts.

The team at Baker Publishing Group and Chosen Books. Dwight Baker, thank you for immediately saying yes and for circumventing pub board (a miracle in itself). Kim Bangs, my editor and friend of three decades. You are a true sister, and your wisdom and compassion precede you. Deirdre Close, Rebecca Shriner, Dan Pitts, Trish Konieczny, and Natasha Sperling—for your excellent work behind the scenes.

Stasz Glinka-Wierzbicki, my interpreter and co-traveler. Your ability to speak four languages was the difference maker, and this book would not have been possible without you. Yuri Safonov, your help on the ground was indispensable. Johnny and Ira Semeniuk and Maryana Kravchenko, your introductions led to many of these stories.

Friends who've always been there—Keith Wall, Tim Peterson, Bill Schultz, Tim Weir, and Mike Greenberg. Benji Horning, who helped kick this whole thing off; Allen Jones, a true brother; Mike, Steve, and the rest of my Wednesday night mates. And fellow writer Rick Killian, who understands.

My co-author, Esther Fedorkevich. Thank you for your partnership, for your support, and for instantly seeing the vision.

A host of praying folks who have lifted us up, including Brent Weidemann, Brad Hirou, Pamela Nishimoto, Israel Hanna, Kay Hiramine, and Patrick Jarvis.

And Jesus, without whom I'd be utterly adrift.

Esther would like to thank . . .

My parents, Paul and Nina Chodniewcz, Ukrainian immigrants who came to the U.S. to raise their family. Thank you for raising us with Ukrainian traditions and values and for providing so many opportunities for your kids.

My husband, Jimmy, and my kids, Alexi Jane and Paul Gregory, for always being there to support me.

There are always so many people behind the scenes making books happen. I'd like to thank my team at The Fedd Agency: Danielle, Kyle, Brittney, Tyler, Alli, Deryn, Tori, Ashley, Ginny, and Katelyn. Thank you for loving books as much as I do.

A big thank-you to the Baker Books team for helping us turn this idea for a project into a beautiful book. For every book sold, I am donating 100 percent of my royalties to Ukrainian families whose lives were impacted during the war.

Historical Ukraine

I f you are unfamiliar with Ukraine's long and eventful history but want to know more, we are including the following time lines. While by no means exhaustive, they cover the country's key historical events from roughly 700 BC through the nineteenth century, and then from the beginning of the twentieth century to the present time.

In Brief: Ukraine's Early History

- 700 BC–200 BC—Ruled by the Scythian kingdom; predating this period, thought to be the region responsible for the domestication of the horse
- 500 BC–AD 500—Roman, Greek, and Byzantine colonies established along the Black Sea
- 370—The Goths are succeeded by the Huns
- 400–500—Early Slavic and Antes peoples, including migrations from areas of present-day Ukraine into Balkans and creation of South Slavic nations
- 650—Bulgar nomadic kingdom

15

- 700—Khazar nomadic kingdom
- 882—Prince Oleg of Novgorod conquers Kyiv and makes it capital of the Rus'
- 882–1240—Golden Age of Kyiv: Kyivan Rus' kingdom included much of present-day Ukraine, Russia, Belarus
- 980–1015—Reign of Vladimir the Great and alignment with Byzantine Christianity
- 1240—Mongol invasion and decline of the Kyivan Rus'
- 1199–1253—Kingdom of Galicia-Volhynia, vassal of the Golden Horde
- 1253–1349—Kingdom of Ruthenia, vassal of the Golden Horde
- 1349–1648—Control by the Polish-Lithuanian Commonwealth
- 1648—Conquest of Kyiv by Cossack Bohdan Khmelnytskyi
- 1648–1764—Cossack Hetmanate
- 1764–1781—Empress of Russia Catherine the Great integrates most of central Ukraine into the Russian Empire; it remains part of Russian Empire until 1917
- 1783—Russian annexation of Crimea from the Crimean Khanate and Tatars
- 1814–1895—Rise of Ukrainian nationalism influenced by Taras Shevchenko and Mykhailo Drahomanov

In Brief: Ukraine since the Twentieth Century

- 1900–1914—An increase in migration throughout Russia; a rise in Ukrainian nationalism

- 1914–1918—World War I sees nearly four million Ukrainians fight for the Imperial Russian Army and the Austro-Hungarian Army
- 1917–1920—Ukrainian People's Republic, short-lived independence after the Bolshevik Revolution of 1917 (February and October revolutions)
- 1917–1921—Ukrainian-Soviet War (War of Independence); several conflicts to assert Ukrainian independence, albeit briefly retained
- 1922—Absorption into newly formed Soviet Union as the Ukrainian Socialist Soviet Republic
- 1920s–1930s—Rise of nationalism and Ukrainization (rise of Ukrainian language and culture)
- 1930–1933—the Holodomor, Soviet famine of 1930–33, kills four million Ukrainians
- 1939–1945—World War II leads to the death of 1.5 million Ukrainian Jews by the Nazis
- 1954—Transfer of control of Crimea from USSR to Ukrainian Socialist Soviet Republic
- 1991—Fall of the USSR and establishment of an independent Ukraine
- 2004–2008—Orange Revolution and power struggle between pro-Western and pro-Russian parties
- November 23, 2013—Euromaidan pro-democracy demonstrations begin in Kyiv
- February 18–23, 2014—Revolution of Dignity leads to the deaths of 121 people
- February 22, 2014—President Viktor Yanukovych flees Kyiv for Russia
- February 20–March 26, 2014—Russian annexation of Crimea
- April 16, 2014–Present—War in Donbas

- May 25, 2014—Petro Poroshenko elected president of Ukraine
- May 20, 2019—Former comedian and television actor Volodymyr Zelensky elected president of Ukraine
- February 24, 2022—Russian invasion of Ukraine

CHAPTER 1

True Stories of Hope for Ukraine

This is a book of true stories captured between late February and late May 2022. I (Kyle) spent three weeks in Poland and western Ukraine in late March and early April interviewing those who had fled the war, as well as aid workers and volunteers. I also conducted numerous interviews with Ukrainians who remain in the country. In compiling the stories, the goal was to give voice to those affected by Russia's February 24, 2022, invasion. In essence, we wanted to get out of the way and let the stories speak for themselves.

My co-author, Esther Fedorkevich, and I did not set out to produce a comprehensive overview of the war in Ukraine, nor do we claim to be military analysts or geopolitical experts. Rather, similar to an ice core sample extracted from a glacier, the stories represent a sliver of history from a specific time and place. Our goal was simple: Tell the stories of real Ukrainians living through the largest and most devastating war in Europe in eight decades.

Esther's maternal Ukrainian grandparents fled religious persecution and Stalin's Holodomor—the man-made famine that killed more than four million Ukrainians—in the early 1930s. Her grandmother and grandfather walked across the border into China, looking for a better life for their children. Her paternal grandparents left Ukraine in 1928, seeking better opportunities in Argentina before emigrating to New Jersey in the 1960s. Esther's husband, Jimmy, is also Ukrainian-American.

My connection to Ukraine is through my adopted son, Jhenya, who was six when my wife, Suzanne, and I adopted him in 2007 from an orphanage in Mariupol. I spent nearly a month there and grew to love the people and culture. Since then, our family has been closely following events in Ukraine—particularly for the past eight years.

Esther and I rejoiced when Ukraine emerged from the Maidan Revolution in early 2014 with a newly formed pro-democracy government, and then we quickly grew concerned when Russia annexed the Crimea a short time later. Our concern turned to deep worry when the War in Donbas broke out. It was yet another connection point for Esther, who has relatives in Ukraine, and for me.

All the people featured in these pages are real, and their stories have been retold as accurately as possible. We often only use first names, and at times names are changed to protect the identities of the speakers. When we do use aliases, we make note of it.

Esther and I are Christians who have a combined fifty-plus years of experience working in faith-based publishing. Yet while some of the stories come from a faith perspective, we did not set out exclusively to pick faith stories. Rather, our intent was to tell the stories of the people I met and interviewed as accurately as they were told to me. Also, proceeds from this book will be donated to aid organizations helping Ukraine's refugees.

The word *Hope* in this book's title can be read as both a noun and a verb. While we believe there is hope for Ukraine, we also believe it's critical to hope and to pray for peace.

Ultimately, we hope this book gives you an intimate glimpse into the lives of some extraordinary people who have endured terrible hardships with grit and grace.

Sláva Ukrayíni! Heróyam sláva!

CHAPTER 2

Dmitriy, Maryana, and Max

With her husband, Dmitriy, still sleeping, Maryana Kravchenko steps onto the balcony of the fifteenth-floor studio apartment they've rented in Zaporizhzhia, in south central Ukraine. She has a panoramic view of a city that has not yet awakened to the news of Russian military invasion.

It's very quiet on the predawn morning of February 24, 2022. Maryana has risen in the dark to pray and has escaped to the balcony for a time of worship. Her heart is heavy, but she prays into that—asking God to soften the heart of a judge who has so far delayed the adoption process of their sixteen-year-old son, Maksim (or Max), on several occasions.

She also prays that the rumors of a Russian invasion of Ukraine will not materialize. Earlier in February the couple had received news back home in Pennsylvania that the Ukrainian judge in their adoption process was finally ready to hear their case. In fact, the judge had agreed to a virtual court date of February 16. Four days before the hearing, however, the judge changed her mind: "You know what? No, you have to come in. I have to see you."

The in-person court date was scheduled to take place on February 16 in the village where Max's orphanage was located, about 120 kilometers west of Zaporizhzhia. On short notice the Kravchenkos made the thousand-mile drive from their home in Bucks County, Pennsylvania, to Tampa, Florida, so Maryana's mom could take care of their three biological children, Esther, Miriam, and Moses. They then boarded a three-legged flight set to arrive in Kyiv on February 14—two days before many U.S. news outlets predicted the war might start. Upon arriving in Amsterdam, they discovered that their Delta flight to Kyiv had been canceled. In fact, many carriers' flights to Ukraine were falling off the departures board at Schiphol International. Fortunately, Ukrainian Airlines was still operating flights, and the couple arrived at Kyiv's Boryspil International Airport later that day.

Upon arrival they received news that the judge had contracted COVID-19, so the in-person court hearing was postponed. Every couple of days the judge would feed them information. "Maybe in a couple more days," she would say. Finally, the judge's secretary called and said the appointment was confirmed for Friday, February 25, at 2:45 p.m.

One more day until this is all over, thinks Maryana as she stares out at a city still asleep, the only sound the low hum of a distant airplane. At first the sound is faint, and Maryana doesn't think anything of it. But then the sound grows louder, and she realizes she's hearing the deep buzz of not one airplane, but several.

She leaves the balcony and tries to wake up her husband. "I hear aircraft," she says to Dmitriy. "Do you think they are war planes?"

"Go back to sleep. It's still dark out," he says. Max is sleeping in an adjacent room. The court has allowed him to spend several days with them, and they've been enjoying the time together.

Maryana glances at her phone lying on the nightstand, alarmed to see several messages from relatives and friends in the United States, some of whom she hasn't talked to in fifteen years. The images in the news links are terrifying—bombs dropping and buildings on fire. As she sits on the edge of the bed, she says, "It's happening, Dmitriy. And I just heard war planes when I was out on the balcony."

Not long after waking up Dmitriy, Maryana receives a call from the court secretary. "The judge wants to see you this morning—it can't wait until tomorrow. You need to get in your car and drive here now."

As they leave Zaporizhzhia with Max to begin the two-and-a-half-hour drive to the courthouse, they pray that the process will go smoothly. They are encouraged by the experience of a neighbor back in Pennsylvania who had adopted from the nearby town of Berdyansk two months earlier. The judge in that case asked the parents two questions and waived the thirty-day waiting period.

Unfortunately, however, as soon as Dmitriy, Maryana, and Max walk into the courtroom, they can tell it's going to be a long morning. The judge immediately sets an aggressive tone. "If this adoption is approved, I'm telling you right now that I will not waive the thirty-day waiting period."

She then starts in on Max, interrogating him belligerently. "Why do you want to go to America with this wealthy couple?" the judge says. At one point she yells at Max and asks if he is being forced to go to the United States against his will. He says no—that he wants to go and that it was his decision—and that he wants to be a part of the Kravchenko family.

The judge then turns her ire on the Kravchenkos. "You must be very wealthy to be here. Are you millionaires?" she says. "Who are you, Pamela Anderson and Tommy Lee? Do you have a live-in nanny? How else can you take care of four children?"

They tell her no, they are not wealthy, and no, they don't have a live-in nanny. And Maryana says, "I am their mom—I will take care of them."

Maryana, originally from Lviv, and Dmitriy, from Odesa, are now U.S. citizens. "It angered her that we were Ukrainians who now live in America," says Dmitriy.

After two hours of grueling questions, the adoption is approved—but the thirty-day waiting period is upheld. The Kravchenkos plead their case, noting that Russia's military invasion has started that very morning, and they just want to get their son someplace safe. Can the judge please waive the thirty-day waiting period?

"Family court has nothing to do with war," the judge snaps back.

It does if you are leaving your son behind, thinks Maryana, stifling the urge to say the words out loud.

Despite their best efforts to convince the judge otherwise, she cannot be swayed. The family now faces a major dilemma: Where will Max go as he waits out the thirty-day period? Maryana confides, "The judge did not want Max to leave Ukraine. She believed that by enforcing the thirty-day waiting period, Max would change his mind—even during wartime, with bombs going off."

Dmitriy, a building contractor, and Maryana, an optometrist, had both arranged two weeks off from their respective jobs. And with three young children waiting for them back in Tampa, their two weeks are running out. They have to make the excruciating decision to leave without Max, as it would be impossible to stay in Ukraine for another month.

Max is one of ten orphaned children, including four younger siblings who live in adoptive families, and four older ones who are independent. Max and his remaining sibling, Bogdan, live in an orphanage and attend a nearby trade school. The Kravchenkos first met Max and Bogdan in December 2018 through an international hosting program. It's a great way for orphans to experience another culture and lifestyle, which also allows prospective parents to get to know potential adoption candidates.

Though Max loved visiting Bucks County, Pennsylvania, and seemed like a natural fit with the Kravchenko family, Bogdan didn't want to return to the United States. Over the next three years, Max would make three more visits to stay with the Kravchenkos. During those visits a deep bond developed between Max, Dmitriy, Maryana, and their three biological children. Bogdan, two years older than Max, had a serious girlfriend and wanted to remain in Ukraine. And due to complexities in the Ukrainian adoption system, Max could not be adopted until his older brother, Bogdan, aged out (turned eighteen).

So the family had to press pause on the adoption while Max stayed in the orphanage, waiting two years until Bogdan's eighteenth birthday. The brothers had a fragmented relationship and argued and fought often. The Kravchenkos did everything they could to try to help Max. They sent shoes, clothes, and other necessities to the orphanage, and they prayed constantly for his safety.

In August 2021 Max's brother turned eighteen and the Kravchenkos were set to pursue Max's adoption. With their dossier complete and fully translated, an October court date was set, which was then delayed until December 4. Due to backlogs in the region's adoption system, COVID-19 complications, and other delays beyond the Kravchenkos' control, all they could do was wait and pray. As December approached, the date was again moved, this time to January 21, 2022. That date was then pushed back to February 16.

A three-and-a-half-year journey came down to this: With war descending upon the Zaporizhzhia area, and the Kravchenkos' inability to stay in-country any longer, mother, father, and newly adopted son might have to say good-bye—once again.

Dmitriy tries one more time, asking the trade school director, "Listen, I have family in Odesa who can look after Max.
Can we take him there?"

"You can," says the director, "but you can go to jail for that."

Exhibiting maturity well beyond his sixteen years, Max says,
"Listen, Dad, we aren't going to break the law. I will be okay.
I am going to stay here and lay low."

"We bought Max a lot of food and said our good-byes,"
says Maryana. "Max had prayed to accept Christ a few days
earlier, while we were all visiting Dmitriy's family in Odesa,
so we prayed together one last time. We understood that the
journey could come to an end right there, and we knew that
we might not see one another until heaven."

Tearing themselves away from this emotional scene, Dmitriy
and Maryana board a train out of Zaporizhzhia, back to Kyiv.
From there, they plan to speed west by car, trying to make it to
the Polish border. Soon, the Ukrainian army is blowing bridges
into Kyiv to slow the Russian assault, so there are few routes out
of the city. Because of these limitations, the traffic is at a near
standstill, and it takes seven hours just to leave Kyiv's outskirts.
Many people are walking or biking out of the city. The couple
can hear bombs going off in the suburbs around Kyiv—places
like Irpin and Bucha—and they can see Ukrainian tanks and
infantry camouflaged just inside the tree line of the forest that
hugs Auto Route E40.

The Kravchenkos had been in touch with the U.S. State Department due to the sensitive nature of things on the ground.
Putin had been massing Russian troops along the Ukrainian
border for some months, and there was wide speculation that an
invasion was imminent. "Once the war actually broke out, the
State Department contacted me," Maryana said. "They said,
'Hello, Maryana, do you and Dmitriy mind leaving Ukraine?'"

It was polite like that, as if the official were asking Maryana
to return a baking dish. Maryana can smile about it now. "I

assured them that we were at that moment headed for the Polish border. It was actually comforting to know that the State Department was able to contact us and check on our safety."

The couple arrived in western Ukraine, and one scene in particular sticks in Maryana's mind. "We roll up to one Ukrainian checkpoint, and it's completely manned by normal Ukrainian guys from the local village. Most were older men in civilian clothes, and it was just comforting to see the solidarity—how the whole country was helping out."

After crossing the border into Poland, they track down a bus that will take them to Warsaw. Dmitriy explains, "When we board the bus the people are looking at me suspiciously. I have to explain that I'm not running from the war, but that I am American. I felt like that guy on the *Titanic* who was the only man in the lifeboat with the women and children." Healthy male Ukrainian citizens between the ages of eighteen and sixty are not allowed to leave the country and are required to fight or serve the war effort in other ways.

In the meantime, Max has taken shelter in his trade school building. Even though it's illegal for him to leave Ukraine for thirty days, all the courthouse workers have fled the country. Even his trade school director has fled to western Ukraine—the same person who warned the Kravchenkos that if they took Max to Odesa, they could be thrown in jail.

Maryana opens her Telegram app and sees a message from Max, telling her that there is a World War II bomb shelter that older folks have rediscovered in the village—it had been used by their family members to hide from the Nazis eighty years earlier. Ukrainian soldiers have just recently arrived and are running out of ammunition. Some of the older villagers show the soldiers where the shelter is, and they dig down to reach the iron doors. A Ukrainian army tank is parked near the shelter entrance. Even Max's brother is in the shelter. "We were praying the Lord's Prayer and reading the New Testament," says Max.

Max gets to know some of the soldiers—some not much older than he is—and one of them says, "Listen, kid, get out while you can." Max asks a friend to take him in a taxi to flee the city. But Max's orphanage director becomes quite upset and tells Max he needs to return to the shelter. So while Max's friend heads to Odesa, Max obeys and returns to the bomb shelter. By this time, news of the shelter has spread in the area, and there are up to five hundred people seeking refuge there.

The brothers are together in the bomb shelter for twelve days. Water and electricity had been knocked out, so a few people go to the local church and ask the Orthodox priest for candles. The church gives them armloads—enough to light the shelter for several days.

As the days go by, Russian artillery strikes intensify. The strikes come in cycles, and the brothers count the hits. At one point Bogdan says, "The next time it starts, we won't have to count to fifteen." The bombing starts and the boys start counting, "One, two, three, four, five, six, seven, eight, nine, ten, eleven . . ." At eleven, they begin to recite the Lord's Prayer, and the bombing stops.

The Kravchenkos contact multiple organizations on the ground in an attempt to exfiltrate Max from his village, which is now a hotly contested war zone. "People are well meaning, but they tell us that it's just too dangerous, and it would be suicide to try to get to them," Dmitriy said.

Max knows that if he goes above ground, he could be killed. The bombing is that intense. And at night, when it's safer to emerge, there is a curfew in place and anyone out past 5:00 p.m. can be shot. So they have to stay put.

Finally, Maryana reaches a war chaplain named Albert Homiak, who works with Republic Pilgrim and its founder, Gennadiy Mokhnenko, in Mariupol (see the story "Gennadiy Mokhnenko" in chapter 11). "These are amazing people who have been working with homeless and orphaned kids in the

Mariupol area for twenty-five years, and who do frontline work with soldiers," says Maryana. Republic Pilgrim has been on the front lines during the eight-year War in Donbas, and is now working around the clock in the heavily bombed city of Mariupol and surrounding areas.

The Kravchenkos speak to Albert, and he says he is in a village not too far from Max that is under heavy attack. Albert tells them that he is very close to Max, but that the entire area is becoming too dangerous. "We can go get your son, but we have to go *now*," says Albert. At that point Albert and his team load up and race toward Max's village. As they drive into a hot war zone, Albert prays loudly, "Lord, protect this vehicle and everyone in it. Let us just live simply on this earth, and let us serve You!"

Dodging Russian positions and small arms fire, they reach Max and also offer to take Bogdan, but he decides to stay. This time when the brothers part, there is no arguing or anger. They hug and Max says his good-byes.

The Kravchenkos have been trying to reach the director at one of the nearby orphanages, but can't get ahold of her. They soon find out that the director there has evacuated 105 younger orphans, leaving Max behind. Maryana understands that the director faced a very difficult decision and had to think of the younger children, especially several with disabilities. "I am just relieved that they all made it to Poland, and are safe now," she offers.

Only one teacher stays behind to look after the kids in the shelter. She has an eighty-seven-year-old mother who cannot leave, so she tells the others, "You should go, but I'm not going anywhere." As Albert and Max prepare to leave, they offer her money for food, but she declines. "I don't need money—there are no more stores. We have food enough for now."

Albert, Max, and the team leave the village and head east, back toward Zaporizhzhia.

Dmitriy picks up the story. "'Where would you like me to take him?' Albert asked us. We instructed him to leave Max in the hands of a local orphanage in Zaporizhzhia where staff said they could help evacuate Max. So he and Max said their good-byes and Albert headed off."

In Zaporizhzhia, the police took Max into their care and dropped him off at the local orphanage, thinking he would be safe there. A bus depot across the street serves as a major transit point for refugees heading west. The orphanage looks deserted behind huge, locked gates. When they approach the gates, a woman appears. "I can keep the boy overnight, and tomorrow I can get him on one of the evacuation buses. I will give him food and a comfortable place to sleep. Don't worry."

Someone must have mentioned that Max is ultimately headed for the United States, because instead of offering hospitality, the woman smelled money and locked him in a room. "She then tells us that she needs money in exchange for Max's release," Maryana says. "So we reach out to the woman and she says, 'I need five thousand dollars and then I will let the child go.'"

Horrified, the Kravchenkos tell her, "You need to let him go—*now!* What you are doing is illegal." But she says that Max is one of her orphans, and that he has no guardian.

They contact Albert, who is still in the Zaporizhzhia area, and he is irate. A widower, Albert has eleven adopted kids of his own and has a huge heart for orphans. So he calls his contacts in Kyiv and arranges for temporary custody of Max. When Albert arrives at the orphanage he screams through the gates, demanding that the woman release Max—which she does.

Albert adds, "At this point I decide that I'm not giving this kid over to anyone else. You work with so many different people, and most of them are trustworthy. . . ." But unfortunately, this woman was not—she was trying to exploit an already horrible situation.

Albert brings Max to a warehouse based out of a Baptist church in Zaporizhzhia, where they're funneling humanitarian aid headed to the eastern front. Many of Albert's sons are working there, and Max pitches in to help. From there, Albert brings Max and others to a town between Ternopil and Lviv, in the relatively safer western part of the country. Albert then escorts Max to Lviv, where shelling has recently hit the outskirts. The Kravchenkos ask if Albert can get him across the border to Poland, but Albert says he can get in a lot of trouble, because the thirty-day waiting period doesn't expire until March 26—two days away.

Max sleeps on a cot in the stairwell of an aid center in Lviv and keeps busy by loading potatoes and other food onto aid vans. On March 26—his last day in Ukraine—Max sees a missile streak across the sky; seconds later it slams into an industrial complex and injures five. It's the first time the Russians have struck Lviv within the city's boundaries. Though the strike occurs only three kilometers away, Max brushes it off when he speaks about it with Maryana. "It's just light bombing, Mom. It's no big deal." And in contrast to what he has been through in the village bomb shelter near Zaporizhzhia, it is light bombing.

Later on the Kravchenkos learn just how bad the artillery strikes were in Max's village. "He did not want to worry us, so when he was underground for those twelve days early in the war, he'd tell us, 'They're bombing a little bit,' when it fact it was nearly nonstop," says Dmitriy.

After Max left the shelter, a missile struck the fourth floor of the trade school, right next to the shelter. There was so much rubble and debris that soldiers had to dig down to access the shelter. Thankfully, no one inside was injured. Today, Max's village is almost completely destroyed.

"Wherever that kid went, it seemed like bombs followed him, as did miracles!" says Dmitriy. "He was always one step ahead of danger, thanks to a lot of prayer and the Lord's mighty work. First, he was near Zaporizhzhia when the nuclear plant was bombed. Then he was in the shelter, where bombs destroyed his village, and finally he was in Lviv the very first day people in the city were injured."

God was in the middle of it, though, and kept reassuring the Kravchenkos that Max was okay. "God was telling us to *wait, this is all in My timing*," says Maryana. "We started to question why God would leave this kid by himself in a war zone, but He reminded us that Jesus waited four days to raise Lazarus. So the glory can only be given to Him."

As the thirty-day waiting period winds down, Maryana and Dmitriy fly from Pennsylvania to Warsaw to make final arrangements to bring Max home. When they land, however, Ukrainian officials say they need a decree stating that the thirty-day waiting period has been fulfilled and that the adoption is official. After the documents arrive a day later, Max is able to pass through the border and travel to Warsaw.

In Warsaw there are standard medical examinations through the U.S. consulate, last-minute paperwork, and the momentous occasion of Max receiving his newly minted U.S. passport.

Five days after he crosses into Poland, I meet Max and the Kravchenkos in Warsaw. Sitting in a quaint Turkish restaurant near Warsaw's main square, we enjoy *döner kebab*, *köfte*, and *baklava*, washed down with prodigious amounts of jet-black tea. I ask Max what it's like to be safe and headed to America.

"I can't really fit it into my mind," he says. "It's hard to comprehend it." Max looks at all the plates of food and grows quiet. "For days we ate very simple meals while we stayed in the bomb shelter. The babushkas cooked macaroni over an open fire. Other days, a single bowl of soup would be the only meal."

Maryana's eyes shine with pride. "The fact that Max went through all that he did, and is with us now, is a miracle. It's proof that no matter what the devil throws at you, God's plan is greater and stronger."

I learn that Max will soon turn seventeen, and I ask him what he wants for his birthday. Without hesitation—and echoing his parents' sentiments—he says, "I just want to be home."

With that, we all raise dark glasses of Turkish tea and toast Maksim Kravchenko, a brave young man with his entire life ahead of him.

CHAPTER 3

The Hunting Lodge

I meet Natasha Olshanska near the Carrefour supermarket, a glittering grocery store inside Warsaw's upscale Galeria Mokotów. Though we've never met, I instantly know it's Natasha when I see her walking toward the entrance to the store. Her pace is quick and she looks determined, in contrast to those around her. It's a Sunday afternoon and throngs of Varsovians casually stroll the mall as they browse shops and sip chai.

For Natasha, though, it's clear that this visit is all business. I walk up and introduce myself, and hope I have the right person. We shake hands and discuss our plan of attack. Today's goal is to purchase food for eight Ukrainian women and children who have fled the war and are living in a nearby two-bedroom apartment. My interpreter, Stasz Glinka-Wierzbicki, helps Natasha grab food items as I push the large grocery cart. It's clear Natasha does this regularly—she knows the layout of the store and the exact items she needs. I can see twenty-three-year-old Stasz's wiry frame up ahead as he darts to gather items from shelves. In fact, it's hard to keep up as I navigate the cart around families and baby strollers.

Between trips to the cart to dump in whole chickens, liters of milk, and cartons of eggs, Natasha explains that she makes this grocery run twice a week for this particular apartment. Grocery shopping sorted, we head back to our parking spot below the cavernous mall. Stasz carefully guides his slightly battered 2000 BMW toward the exit, and we finally extricate ourselves from the bowels of the mall.

On the drive to the apartment building, Natasha explains that this particular group of women and their daughters—between the ages of seventy-five and one—are from a few different towns in Ukraine, including Kyiv. The common thread is that they all know Natasha or her business colleague, Yuri Safonov. Natasha is an adoption facilitator and translator who helps arrange hosting visits for orphans in the United States and Canada. The hosted kids—typically ages seven to sixteen—experience a different culture while prospective adoptive parents get to know a child. It is often a win-win.

Yuri is the reason I've met Natasha. I probably wouldn't be in Poland—or writing this book for that matter—if not for Yuri, who was our adoption facilitator fifteen years earlier when my family and I adopted our son, Jhenya (see "Jhenya," chapter 12). Due to Yuri's mastery of the Ukrainian adoption system, our family's experience was nearly seamless. That's saying a lot in a country where the process often sputters and stalls and where judges can be capricious.

Over the years, Yuri and I kept in touch through social media, and when the bombing started in Kyiv, where he lives, we communicated regularly. He and his wife, Alesia, and their one-year-old daughter, Emily, were sheltering with others in the basement of their apartment. After mulling their options, Yuri decided to get his wife and baby out. Over four harrowing days they drove to Vinnytsia, then Khmelnytskyi, and on to Lviv. From there, Yuri arranged safe passage to Warsaw—to the apartment where we are about to deliver groceries. Meanwhile, Yuri remains in Ukraine, continuing his efforts to evacuate orphans.

Alesia and baby Emily greet Natasha, Stasz, and me at the door of the apartment they temporarily share with six other women and girls. Like more than seven million fellow Ukrainians who have fled the country, they don't know how long they will be here, or where they will go next. We manage to jam into the small kitchen as two of the older ladies offer us tea and cakes. The atmosphere is talkative and spirited. Natasha bounces baby Emily as the ladies talk about her recent first birthday, celebrated here in Poland and apart from Dad.

After we say our good-byes, it's back to the grocery store to buy snacks and staples for the orphans and caretakers at the home where Natasha and her sixteen-year-old son, Jhenya, have been staying for several days. This time, rather than chickens and eggs, we leave with more than three hundred dollars' worth of fruits and snacks to accommodate eighteen orphans. In all, including caretakers like Larisa, who works closely with Natasha, twenty-four people share a large house on the outskirts of Mińsk Mazowiecki, about thirty kilometers east of Warsaw.

This group is comprised mostly of children from an orphanage in Vinnytsia, but a few are from other places such as Odesa and Khmelnytskyi. When you turn off the local village road through the narrow walled entrance to the residence, it's a step back in time. A long, straight lane flanked by towering linden trees leads to a circular driveway in front of a stately white house. I learn that a lot of work has gone into the 150-year-old hunting lodge, which had stood empty for the last few years.

Natasha and Yuri worked closely with a Texas-based orphan-hosting organization called International Host Connection (IHC) to find the old manor house. The Partner Group, a local real estate company that owns the property, donated the use

37

of the home to the refugees. A small army worked around the clock to renovate the home, bringing in furniture, kitchen appliances, toys, clothes, customized children's bunk beds, and ten thousand dollars' worth of computers to assist the older kids who would be attending school remotely.

In less than two weeks the empty manor house was transformed and ready for the orphans and their caregivers. "All of the money and supplies were donated by the Partner Group," says Tasha Bradley, founder of IHC. Ukrainians who themselves had just recently fled the war worked alongside local volunteers, Tasha tells me over a Zoom call from her home in Prosper, Texas.

Though it's early April there's more than a foot of snow on the ground, and Stasz's BMW slides a bit before jerking to a stop in front of the hunting lodge. We are immediately greeted by several kids, including two-year-old Kolya, who takes a shine to Stasz's Sony a7iii mirrorless camera. It's not a cheap device, but Kolya handles it like a boss, even snapping some excellent photos.

We remove our boots and set them at the end of a long, neat line of children's shoes along the foyer wall, and place our jackets on a fat coat rack laden with little coats and hats. Other kids gather round as we unload the groceries, and Natasha has them line up to receive a pre-dinner treat. It's clear by their behavior that Natasha runs a tight ship—they wait in single file, hands out, all smiles. The house is bright and inviting, and the smell of hot borsch and bread greets us as we sit at the twenty-foot-long dining table. Natasha's son, Jhenya, bring us hot black tea and snacks. A light snow begins to fall as the sun sets.

During dinner I learn that Natasha lost her husband to cancer two years before, and life was starting to return to normal when the war broke out. Mother and son left their town of Khmelnytskyi to help evacuate 120 children from the Nest, an orphanage in Vinnytsia in southwestern Ukraine.

When the group's train arrived in Lviv, the bus they had prearranged was nowhere to be found, so they had to scramble. Their new bus didn't have a bathroom, and the little food and water they had would have to do. After all, the one-hundred-kilometer drive from Lviv to the Polish border normally takes just ninety minutes.

In fact, it took Natasha's group eighteen hours to cross the border. Natasha was up all night on the bus, taking kids into the nearby trees to go to the bathroom. And after a while, the group ran out of food and water. Determined to keep the miles-long line of vehicles moving, Natasha and Larisa took turns knocking on car windows to wake up sleeping drivers.

After dinner we clear dishes and enjoy small cakes and more tea. The children are settled on rugs and blankets in the large living room, watching a Ukrainian children's DVD. A mountain of neatly stacked toys sits against a far wall. At 8:00 p.m. sharp the television is turned off and the kids promptly leave the room with hardly a word. I've never seen a group of children respond to a bedtime call without a single complaint. All eighteen little ones disappear to brush teeth and listen to bedtime stories.

As the caregivers prepare the younger kids for bedtime, the teenagers and a few of the adults settle down on the comfortable couches lining one wall of the living room. The amber light from a single lamp spills against the window, illuminating snowflakes tapping against the glass. Most of the teens have been fairly quiet up to this point, but open up as the evening draws on. Stasz and I meet Masha from Odesa (see "Tatiana, Bogdan, and Masha," chapter 14), brothers Max and Artem, Vasya, and Veronika, who are from Vinnytsia. Masha's mom, Tatiana, and Jhenya join us as well.

Like fallen leaves swept together by the winds of war, we've gathered on a snowy night in the Polish countryside to hear stories that are gut-wrenching and searing. For these six teenagers—ranging in age from twelve to seventeen—it seems a lifetime's worth of experiences compacted into six short weeks. Their stories include destruction, ash, and fragment, inexorably compressed into hard, sharp diamonds of loss and uncertainty. But like fine details illuminated by a jeweler's loupe, their stories also reveal more subtle cuts that refract hope and strength.

According to Max and Artem's adoptive mom, Lisa, their court hearing at 5:30 p.m. on the eve of February 24 was likely the last adoption approved by the Ukrainian government before the adoption system shut down. Max is an avid soccer player, and Artem is intelligent and thoughtful, asking me a lot of questions about a typical school day in the United States. About a week after I met Max and Artem their adoptive parents arrived. Their journey to the United States was in limbo, however, as they waited in Warsaw for paperwork to clear. Finally, weeks later I heard that the necessary red tape had been cut and that they are now starting their new life in Texas.

Masha is vibrant and creative and asks me questions about the writing process. She attends Ukrainian high school remotely and shows me videos of acting roles she has landed. Jhenya is tall with jet-black hair, intelligent eyes, and a quiet intensity. The next day he will attend his first day of public school here in Poland, and he's a little nervous. "The classes will be in Polish, and I am just learning the language," he confides. I learn from his mom that he has actually only been speaking Polish for three weeks, but he has already gained a foundation. As well as attending Polish school, he also has a couple of Ukrainian classes to finish. He's often up past midnight with homework.

When I first met seventeen-year-old Vasya earlier that afternoon, he was quiet and stood on the opposite side of the room. But tonight he opens up, and I learn that he's an accomplished guitarist who is in the process of being adopted by a family in Florida (see "Vasya," chapter 17).

Veronika is quiet as well, and on this first night, she just sits nearby and listens. Over the next few days, however, her vivacious personality emerges, and we learn that she's a lightning-fast striker on her Vinnytsia football club. She's also the house's appointed hairstylist, her skills evidenced by several of the children's recent haircuts.

All these teens—except Masha and Jhenya—have spent much of their lives in Ukraine's orphanage system. Thankfully, most of them are in various stages of the adoption process, a system that has ground to a halt, however, at least until the war is over.

It's growing late, but Stasz and I don't want to leave. Not wanting to wear out our welcome, I had put my shoes on an hour earlier but took them off again as the conversation regained momentum. Just before midnight we say good-bye and promise to return the next day for another visit.

The one day that we had planned to stay in Mińsk Mazowiecki turns into four. Our days are filled with trips to the shoe store and supermarket, and a long afternoon of sightseeing and shopping in downtown Warsaw. We also find a racquet club that has a bright café with a pool table and huge TV screen showing European football matches. We take the teenagers along, and it's gratifying to watch them enjoy a hamburger and play billiards. They thank us for getting them out of the house. Masha confides, "We love the little ones, but it's hard to be with them 24/7!"

Each evening, Stasz and I return to our hotel after a busy day with the kids and discuss whether we should leave for the border the next day. Inevitably, we remember that this child or that still needs shoes, so moving on isn't yet an option.

On day four it is time to say good-bye.

Before we leave the hunting lodge Natasha hands me a small toy dragon with blue and yellow stripes, matching the colors of the Ukrainian flag. She says, "This is so you remember to pray for Ukraine—and to pray for homes for all the children."

Weeks later, back in San Diego, the plastic dragon keeps watch from the edge of my desk. Its wings are raised, perpetually poised for flight. I often look at it and think about twenty-four people in a Polish hunting lodge who taught me that joy can be found even amid life's toughest circumstances. But even more, that in choosing such joy, one exhibits the purest form of courage.

CHAPTER 4

At the Gates of Mariupol

Mariupol.

Fifty years from now when historians recount the brutal war Russia waged against Ukraine, perhaps more than any other city, Mariupol is the one our great-grandchildren will talk about. Novels will be written and films will be made. It will be to Europe in the twenty-first century what Stalingrad was in the twentieth. A city synonymous with brutality, death, and destruction, but also defiance, courage, and survival in the face of desperate odds. But Mariupol will also retain historical significance because even before 2014, when Russia's war in Ukraine actually started, it was a strategic target for Vladimir Putin—for several reasons.

Many people outside Ukraine had never heard of Mariupol before February 24, 2022. As the war broke out and the news footage rolled in, however, it became increasingly clear that Mariupol was suffering in ways most of us found unimaginable in modern-day Europe. Civilian buildings, including apartment complexes, hospitals, and theaters sheltering children, were bombed indiscriminately. No electricity or running water;

dwindling food supplies; the dead either piled in the street or burned to reduce the chance of disease. Children drinking from rain puddles as their mothers cooked over small fires in bombed-out stairwells. Up to twenty thousand civilians killed.

What Russia's military had done in Syria in the previous decade was happening in cities like Mariupol: a scorched-earth policy that has damaged or leveled ninety percent of the city's buildings and left it in ruins.[1]

For those paying close attention, however, even before 2014 Mariupol and the rest of southeastern Ukraine increasingly became a region upon which Putin was setting his sights. In the lead-up to the 2014 Winter Olympics in Sochi, Russia, rumors flew of Putin's designs to "reclaim" the Crimean Peninsula, just 250 kilometers west of Mariupol. And sure enough, shortly after the Olympics ended, Russian troops—dressed in plain uniforms and driving unmarked military vehicles—made an amphibious landing on Crimea's shores to take control of the picturesque peninsula on the Black Sea, annexing it from Ukraine.

This despite the fact that Crimea had been transferred to Ukraine sixty years earlier by the Soviet Union. At that time, the USSR's Presidium of the Supreme Soviet decreed that Crimea was to be transferred to the Soviet Republic of Ukraine to "evince the boundless trust and love the Russian people feel toward the Ukrainian people."[2] Behind the hyperbole was a tactical move by Nikita Khrushchev to shore up support in Ukraine in his bid to consolidate power after Stalin's death in 1953.

According to Mark Kramer, director of the Cold War Studies program at Harvard University and a senior fellow of Harvard's Davis Center for Russian and Eurasian Studies, the transfer proceedings included sentiments that are cryptic in light of Russia's 2014 annexation of Crimea. Kramer notes,

> One of the ironies of the transfer of Crimea to Ukraine in 1954 is that when the chairman of the Presidium of the USSR

Supreme Soviet, Kliment Voroshilov, offered his closing remarks at the session on 19 February 1954, he declared that "enemies of Russia" had "repeatedly tried to take the Crimean peninsula from Russia and use it to steal and ravage Russian lands." He praised the "joint battles" waged by "the Russian and Ukrainian peoples" as they inflicted a "severe rebuff against the insolent usurpers." Voroshilov's characterization of Russia's past "enemies" seems eerily appropriate today in describing Russia's own actions vis-à-vis Ukraine. A further tragic irony of the Crimean transfer is that an action of sixty years ago, taken by Moscow to strengthen its control over Ukraine, has come back to haunt Ukraine today.[3]

The world's response to Russia's invasion of the former Soviet republic of Georgia in 2008 had been fairly mild, which led Putin to believe that the annexation of Crimea would be straightforward. And for the most part, it was. Though sanctions were applied, the response from Europe and the West was vocal but lacked teeth.

The annexation took place not long after a pro-Western Ukrainian government in Kyiv emerged from the flames of the Euromaidan protests in late 2013 and early 2014, and the Maidan Revolution that followed in February 2014. (See "Johnny and Ira," chapter 7, for more on the Maidan Revolution.) By the time the barricades were dismantled, Ukraine had ousted its pro-Russian president, Viktor Yanukovych, and had taken a bold step closer to alignment with Western Europe and the United States.

Alarmed by Ukraine's sudden shift to the West, and emboldened by the successful annexation of Crimea, Putin saw a chance to gain a further foothold in southeastern Ukraine. Russia now set its sights on the oblasts (regions) of Donetsk and Luhansk—an area known as the Donbas. Part of Ukraine's rich industrial heartland, the Donbas is made up of a Russian-speaking majority with close ties to their giant neighbor to the east. In 2008 Ukrainian parliamentary elections, for example, the pro-Russian Party of Regions gained about fifty percent of the vote in the two oblasts.

After Maidan, separatist and anti-government tensions rose in the Donbas and soon turned into protests that spread quickly through the region. Backed by Russian arms and training, fighting there soon erupted between the separatists and the Ukrainian army.

Prior to February 24 the Kremlin repeatedly denied direct military involvement in the Donbas, even though there was evidence that Russia was not only sending in weapons, but troops. In fact, in late 2019 a U.K.-based digital forensics agency called Forensic Architecture released damning evidence proving that in summer 2014 Russian troops had taken part in fighting around Ilovaisk, in eastern Ukraine.[4] This is just one case among many verified Russian military actions in the Donbas.

Of course, all pretense of Kremlin denials vanished on February 24, 2022, when the Russian army entered Ukraine on several fronts, including the Donbas region.

And that brings us back to the city of Mariupol, and its critical importance to Russia, and why it has been on Putin's mind for quite some time. Ukraine knows the geographical and economic importance of Mariupol, so that is where the Ukrainian army made its stand in the War in Donbas. In the lead-up to Russia's latest invasion in February 2022, in fact, Mariupol was the front line in the south for the Donbas war, with both armies dug in along a massive network of trenches and redoubts.

In 2007, my family and I found ourselves in Mariupol in a quieter, more peaceful time. As I mentioned in chapter 1, we had traveled there to adopt our son, Jhenya, and I spent nearly a month there. Even then, the citizens of Mariupol talked warily about their superpower neighbor, just sixty kilometers to the east. And while sentiments were mixed back in 2007—many in that part of Ukraine at the time were equally wary of both Putin and Ukrainian nationalism—the people I spoke with just wanted to live peacefully with Russia.

I paused on a tree-lined street one hot August afternoon on that trip to enjoy a cold cup of *kvas*, a delicious, fermented drink made from rye bread. My apartment had no Wi-Fi, so each day I made the two-mile round-trip walk to the closest Internet café, located just off popular Prospekt Mira (Peace Avenue). I had seen the old Toyota trucks towing large painted metal barrels with the word квас painted in Cyrillic on the side, and wondered what they were about.

I bought my *kvas* for twenty-five *hryvnia*—about eighty cents—and sat on a nearby bench to enjoy it in the shade of large birch trees. A man who looked to be in his early sixties—wiry, smartly dressed, with short-cropped salt-and-pepper hair and beard—struck up a conversation. He easily pegged me as American—in my cargo shorts, Chuck Taylors, and UCLA T-shirt—and asked me where I was from. Mariupol doesn't get a lot of American visitors.

Even though our exchange took place fifteen years ago, I remember our brief conversation because he said something that struck me. As we chatted about Mariupol and its proximity to Russia, he said, "As long as the bear stays in its den, we are safe. But the bear grows hungrier every day."

Seven years later, in March 2014, the bear left its den, and for eight years it has been clawing for territory in the Donbas. Ukrainians I interviewed say that Russia's failed plan to capture Kyiv and topple the Ukrainian government was not Putin's primary goal—it would have simply been an added bonus to the higher priority of capturing the Donbas.

Some experts argue that Russia will not be satisfied with stopping if it secures a land corridor across southeastern Ukraine. It's speculated that Putin could press west from Crimea to try to capture Odesa, which would essentially cut off Ukraine from all its ports and critical trade access to the Black Sea. Though the country could still move exports by train through its NATO neighbors to the west, trade would be severely hampered.

From Odesa, there are also fears that Russia will invade Moldova, which is not part of NATO. As well, currently about 1,500 Russian troops are stationed in Transnistria, a tiny breakaway republic that is internationally recognized as part of Moldova. Transnistria hugs a long sliver of land between the Dniester River and the Ukraine-Moldova border. Only time will tell.

As of December 2021, the Donbas conflict had claimed the lives of more than 14,000 troops combined, and more than 3,400 civilians.[5] Those numbers have skyrocketed since Russia's latest phase of the war began on February 24, 2022. It's estimated that between 15,000 and 22,000 Russian soldiers perished in just the first two months of this latest phase of the war.

Like any nation, Ukraine is not perfect. It has its fair share of graft, corruption, and extremism. But the optimal word here is *nation*. It has been a sovereign independent nation now for thirty years, and it deserves to remain so.

Just as we pray for other nations where people are suffering from military conflict—Syria, Afghanistan, South Sudan, and Yemen, among others—we are called to pray for the suffering people of Ukraine. My specific prayer is that peace would come quickly to the nation I have come to know and love. I also pray that cities like Mariupol would soon welcome back quiet days where a cup of *kvas* can be enjoyed peacefully between new acquaintances and old friends alike.

CHAPTER 5

Walking Away from War

I t's April 7, 2022, and we've reached the Poland-Ukraine border. The first things you notice when you walk toward the border crossing at Medyka, Poland, are the colorful tents. They line both sides of a five-meter-wide paved path that stretches for about one hundred meters. As you walk down the narrow passageway, refugees, aid workers, and volunteers talk in a mix of languages—I count ten within the first half hour.

Aid workers sport yellow vests with their group's name printed on the back: the Egyptian Red Cross; Khalsa Aid India; NATAN from Israel; Operation Blessing and Samaritan's Purse from the United States; the International Red Cross; UNICEF; the Red Crescent—among others. The world has come to aid the flood of Ukrainians—mostly women, children, and the elderly—crossing to safety.

In contrast to the war horrors happening less than one hundred kilometers away, this is a corridor of hope. There is collective effervescence—a shared sense of purpose that flows through the crowd and manifests in acts of kindness. In a tent to my right a mom with a stroller sits with a toddler in her lap, eating hot soup. A few feet in front of me two big Italian guys help carry luggage for an elderly couple walking arm in arm. Just ahead of the Italians a cluster of young women huddles around a table where they receive free SIM cards and a tutorial on how to make calls in Poland.

My Polish interpreter, Stasz, and I have come to interview refugees and aid workers at the war's busiest border crossing. Of the more than 3.5 million Ukrainians who have fled the war into Poland, hundreds of thousands have crossed here—by bus, car, and foot. In fact, this is the busiest pedestrian crossing point from Ukraine into Poland.

After leaving the humanitarian corridor we walk a couple of hundred meters toward a trim redbrick building that serves as the immigration office for travelers crossing by foot from Medyka into the village of Shehyni, Ukraine. A full military kit—dark green backpack and daypack—rests against a railing, and a grizzled man bristling with tattoos stands nearby.

Sean (not his real name) is a Royal Marines veteran from Glasgow who has come to fight with the International Legion of Ukraine, comprised of more than twenty thousand foreign fighters. "Two men raped my partner six years ago. She was eight months pregnant and we lost the baby," he says. They broke up soon after.

Sean couldn't sit at home after seeing news stories of Russian soldiers raping Ukrainian women. I ask him how long he plans to be in Ukraine, and he says, "I don't plan to come back." Before I can get clarification, his ride into Ukraine arrives and he gathers his kit and says good-bye.

As a side note, in early June 2022 I reconnected with Sean. After being deployed to the eastern front, he watched one of his friends get his head blown off by an artillery shell, which caused complex post-traumatic stress disorder in Sean. He was medically discharged from the International Legion and returned to Scotland. Prior to traveling to Ukraine in early April, however, he had donated everything he owned to a Ukrainian relief organization. He now struggles to find housing and work, and everything he owns is in his military kit. "The waiting period for Scottish government housing for a single man is several years," he tells me. "But the sacrifice was worth it and is one I would make again."

Stasz—who also speaks Russian, Ukrainian, and English—can't cross with me because he has left his international passport at home. So today it's just me and Google Translate crossing into Ukraine.

I am surprised to see a short queue of Ukrainians with suitcases and children in tow also crossing into their country. Despite the continuing threat of Russian shelling, the towns around Kyiv have been liberated by the Ukrainian army, and these folks are headed back. Some fled with small children, making the difficult choice to leave elderly or non-ambulatory relatives behind. One man says he is returning simply because he wants to be in his own home. When I ask him if it's safe, he says, "I'd rather die in my home than live alone in another country. And I have two dogs waiting for me."

The Polish immigration officer asks me two questions, scans my passport, and stamps it for exit. From there, it's a three-hundred-meter walk up a fenced corridor about three meters wide, capped by barbed wire. This is the Grey Zone—the area between the borders. A couple of minutes later I'm standing at the Ukrainian immigration window.

The female Ukrainian soldier looks at my American passport for about ten seconds, and stamps it. "Da," she says as she taps my birth date. I am welcome here. Despite the fact that I am not carrying a military kit, I believe she thinks I've come to join the International Legion. (I'm fifty-nine, so just under the age limit of sixty.)

"I'm writing a book about the war," I say. But she doesn't understand me. No questions asked, I'm in Ukraine.

I should say, I'm back in Ukraine for the first time since we had come fifteen years ago to pursue adopting Jhenya. We completed the adoption in August 2007, and he is now twenty-one. On that trip, we spent a few days in a flat right off Maidan Square in Kyiv, and then traveled via Donetsk to the southeastern port city of Mariupol. My son's orphanage was in a leafy neighborhood east of the city, and each day's visit took us past the Azovstal iron and steel works, with its massive smokestacks and factory buildings. Azovstal was the sight of the "Ukrainian Alamo," where more than twenty-four hundred Ukrainian soldiers withstood nearly three months of constant shelling before surrendering to Russian forces on May 20, 2022. And Mariupol has been ground to dust.

It's surreal to be back on Ukrainian soil under such starkly different circumstances. I'm now in far western Ukraine, more than one thousand kilometers from Mariupol and Donetsk, where my family and I had been. When I last visited in 2007 Donetsk was a lovely regional capital with streets adorned with tidy flower beds, attractive stores, and bustling restaurants. The two-hour drive from Donetsk to Mariupol was quiet and bucolic, a landscape of sunflower fields and sleepy villages. In 2014, when the War in Donbas broke out, the charming Donetsk airport was decimated during the worst fighting and reduced to rubble. And nearly all of Mariupol's buildings have been damaged or destroyed since Russia's February 2022 invasion.

I exit the small immigration office and head toward another row of humanitarian tents offering food, water, and directions to refugees in transit. I hear English in a tent run by Youth With A Mission, one of the world's largest Christian youth organizations, and I stop to chat with a middle-aged volunteer named Allen from Ohio. He's been at the border for a month, cooking food, helping the elderly, and carrying luggage for weary travelers.

Allen tells me that a week earlier a girl of about twelve came through in a wheelchair. At first he thought the blue streak on her cheek was chalk, as many children wear patriotic blue and yellow face paint. Instead, he realized, it was a jagged scar from a gunshot wound in the process of healing.

It turns out she was the same girl featured in a CNN report from March 25, 2022, that made international headlines. She had been shot twice in the face by Russian soldiers as her family tried to flee Mariupol by car on March 16. "It was the first time I'd seen the physical effects of the war on a child," Allen says. A few weeks earlier the line to cross by foot from Ukraine into Poland was thirty hours long, with night temperatures well below freezing. Two babies had died of exposure.

"I've also seen the effects on dogs," he says.

I ask him to clarify.

"Lots of people have brought their pets with them, and I haven't seen one dog without its tail between its legs."

This thoroughfare—about three meters wide and thirty meters long, with tents on both sides—is the first thing to greet Ukrainians who arrive by bus and make the rest of the short crossing by foot. Though not as long as the aid corridor on the Polish side, it's a wonderful sight for war-weary travelers.

As I look around at the stream of Ukrainians moving past me I notice the dogs for the first time. A wide mix of breeds, some on leads and others in carriers. Not a single tail is wagging.

I enter the border village of Shehyni, buses and taxis filling the main road—Ukraine's Auto Route M11—which leads to Lviv, about seventy-five kilometers due east. Bars and kiosks serve drinks and sandwiches along the broad road as Ukrainians head toward the pedestrian border crossing from the nearby bus station. I follow the sidewalk down the street and away from the border—against a stream of exhausted people pushing suitcases, wheelchairs, and strollers.

The crowds disappear within a few hundred meters of the border. The road is dotted with modest but pleasant homes, small gardens with fresh shoots breaking the soil. A few people sit on their porches to enjoy a pleasant spring day in the sixties. It's hard to believe bombs are falling just seventy-five kilometers away in the picturesque medieval town of Lviv.

I walk about two kilometers and the houses thin out. Down a side road a house is under construction. It's fully framed and the brick walls are half erected. A pallet of bricks sits next to a wheelbarrow, a shovel resting against it. This hopeful domestic scene contrasts starkly with the mass destruction ripping apart much of the rest of the country. A cat skirts around a car and into a hedge as a dog barks in the distance.

An elderly woman emerges from her home and tells me I should go no farther down the road. I reach into my pocket and show her my American passport, and make my retreat. I smile, apologize, and head back to the main road. She nods and seems to relax a bit. Everyone is on edge—even here in a small village tucked right up against the relative safety of NATO's eastern front. I experience a flush of embarrassment, a foreigner who has disturbed local sensitivities.

As I head back toward the border I pass a large house with a temporary sign that reads *World Central Kitchen*, with aid workers relaxing on the front steps. WCK has a big presence on both sides of the border. Started by celebrity chef José Andrés in 2010 after the Haiti earthquake, WCK now serves meals to war-struck and disaster areas around the world. (Later, after I cross back into Ukraine, one of their cooks hands me a cup of their hot soup. I explain that I am not a refugee, but rather a writer doing research for a book. He says, "But you still look hungry." I was, and the soup was delicious.)

I reenter the humanitarian corridor and find myself at the end of the queue of people waiting to pass through Ukrainian immigration on their way to Poland. I help a family with their bags as the line begins to move, and I begin a conversation with a girl named Anna, who is about ten. Through Anna's tentative English and the wonder of Google Translate, I learn that she is with her mother, grandmother, aunt, and younger sister.

They are from Kharkiv, on the far northeastern side of Ukraine. Between them they have two carry-on rolling suitcases and several grocery bags. The wheels on one of the suitcases have broken off, so I pick up the case every time the line moves. The women carry the weight of a battered city on their haggard faces. Their clothes are clean but hard-worn. Pink socks peek through two nickel-sized holes at the tips of Anna's beaten sneakers. The beatific face of Snow White looks up from the back of a small toy chair peeking out of one of her bags, the price sticker visible on the shiny pink plastic. The legs have broken through the bottom of the bag, which Anna sets down with care each time the line moves.

Anna's dad and uncle stayed behind to fight with the Territorial Defense, comprised of volunteer militias created during the War in Donbas. Her family sheltered in their apartment's basement for more than thirty days before they decided to leave. For the past eighteen hours they have been on a train across Ukraine. As night fell everyone was instructed to keep their phones off to enforce a total blackout. With trains coming under fire, darkness offers a veneer of safety.

The line moves, and I pick up the suitcase and shuffle forward five feet. "*Duzhe tobi dyakuyu,*" the mother says. We share some trail mix that I bought at a big box store before leaving home. Anna sifts excitedly through the raisins and almonds to extract the chocolate candies from her packet. It's probably just the familiarity of the scene, or maybe just seeing a ten-year-old kid get excited about a couple of small candies, but I'm hit by a wave of emotion. I manage to hold it together as Anna passes a packet of trail mix to her younger sister.

An hour has passed and we've moved about forty feet. I try to peer over heads in front of me, but the queue disappears into a large white plastic tent with the letters *UNHCR* on the side, the UN Refugee Agency. I can't tell how far we have to go, or how long it will take. Before I had headed across, Stasz had asked two Ukrainian women just entering Poland how long it had taken them to cross. Two or three hours, they said.

By about 4:30 p.m. we reach the entrance to the first of three UN tents. Each tent is about fifty feet wide and one hundred feet long. I think, *Two hours to go one hundred feet, and I'm guessing about three hundred feet to go. So, six more hours?*

The first thing you notice when you enter the tent is the familiar smell of grass and dirt. Family members hold their place in line as loved ones stretch out on the ground. Volunteers circulate with sandwiches, bottles of water, and a huge box of small stuffed animals for the children.

A man dressed in black shirt and white clerical collar walks forward with an acoustic guitar and starts singing in Ukrainian. It's hard to know if he's Ukrainian Orthodox or a pastor from another denomination. People throughout the crowd begin to sing along, some raising their hands in the air with eyes closed. There is a sense of relief, and the song seems to brighten the collective mood. After a few songs, the singer pauses and yells, *Sláva Ukrayíni!* while the crowd shouts back, *Sláva Ukrayíni! Heróyam sláva!* Glory to the heroes, indeed—many of whose parents, spouses, and children are standing in this queue with me.

The guitar pastor is then joined by exuberant twenty-somethings from a Christian group called Awakening Europe (AE). A tall, thin American man with long blond hair asks through a female interpreter if there's anyone in the crowd who would like prayer. Several people come forward, and AE team members stand in small clusters, praying for people of all ages. The line inches forward. I mechanically pick up the broken suitcase and move it another five feet. Anna returns from a prayer group, clutching a coloring book of Bible stories and a fistful of crayons. She and her sister sit on their backpacks and patiently take turns adding colors to the Ark and the animals two-by-two.

The line stops moving. No one seems to know why. A good thirty minutes go by before we move another few feet. One item noticeably absent from the tent is toilets. I'm told that to use the bathroom you have to walk back to the aid tents where there's a bank of portables. I see moms with kids in hand walking back and forth from that direction.

There's a small commotion behind me, and just as I turn to see what's going on, a brown-and-white Jack Russell terrier shoots past me toward the front of the line. Kids try to catch the dog as it races by, but it escapes and skirts through the crowd.

We exit the first tent around 6:00 p.m., and I figure I'm about a third of the way through the queue. So, three and a half hours down, and probably five or so to go. There's a gap of about thirty feet between these first two tents, and several adults steal a quick cigarette before we enter the second tent. There's murmuring up ahead, and I see a few people move to the side. There's the Jack Russell again, shooting back in the opposite direction. Why is the dog in such a hurry? Who owns it? Or is it sort of a border mascot? It zips past me again.

Two muzzled Dobermans sit next to their female owner along the edge of the tent—a thirty-something Angelina Jolie–looking woman dressed in a black pantsuit with a Louis Vuitton bag at her feet. Two women in their seventies stand near her in rough work boots, wool skirts, worn brown coats, and colorful headscarves, each flanked by large, weathered shopping bags. One holds a teacup Chihuahua as small as a kitten. She places the dog on the ground, and the Dobermans nuzzle it as it darts between their legs. The two older women strike up a lively conversation with Ms. Jolie.

Most of the people around me are from Kharkiv, Ukraine's second-largest city, which has seen some of the fiercest and bloodiest fighting in the war. Just thirty kilometers from the Russian border, it has been a high-level target for Russia from day one of the invasion. I'm not a war reporter; I've never been to a war zone before. Sitting here among Kharkiv's citizens is a visceral experience. There's a sense of anticipation over leaving a war zone, muted by the fresh trauma everyone has been through. It's like attending a wedding and funeral at the same time.

One gentleman in his thirties uses my phone's Google Translate app to share his story. He speaks with emotion, enunciating each word. He hands the phone back to me, and I read the English translation: *I didn't want to leave my apartment because me and an older man were the only people left and were taking care of the dogs and cats left behind in the building. But when the bombing got worse, he told me to go, and that he had lived a full life and that he felt purpose taking care of his little zoo.*

After I finish reading, the young man taps his chest and in halting English says, "Heart hurt."

But while these people are victims of this brutal war, they do not comport themselves as such. They are clearly exhausted physically, emotionally, and mentally, but there is a buoyancy in their words and body language. They help each other with luggage, share food, and talk in small groups. There's a quiet hopefulness as they wait to enter a country where they can sleep without the specter of sirens or shelling. Collective effervescence.

"We did what we had to do for our families," says a silver-haired man named Vasya. "We are here by God's grace and are the fortunate ones," he adds. Once settled in Poland, he plans to volunteer to help bring humanitarian goods into Ukraine. I ask him if he is concerned about reentering a war zone. "No, because those are my people and that is my country. Even if the Russians destroy every single house, it will never be theirs."

It's about 9:00 p.m. and the line has slowed considerably. I've made it to the end of the second tent, with one to go. I'm six feet two and can see over the crowd. After the third tent the line chicanes toward a set of glass double doors that lead into Ukrainian immigration. Soup, hot sandwiches, and cups of hot tea circulate, provided by aid workers from the Red Crescent, Operation Blessing, World Central Kitchen, and a group from Israel.

"Zip" the Jack Russell blasts past me again, a bit of sandwich in its mouth. Anna and her sister laugh. They are smiling, and their mother and grandmother take notice. I recognize the word *posmikhatysya* in their conversation, which means "smile." Now mother and grandma are smiling too.

As we inch closer to the end of the third tent, a Ukrainian police officer moves toward us carrying a new rolling suitcase. Excitedly, Anna's mom grabs the broken suitcase I've been hauling and carries it out of the line. This police officer heard about their hobbled suitcase and has procured a replacement. Anna and her mom carefully open the broken suitcase and transfer their possessions to the new one. The family is elated, and we joke that they no longer need me as their *v'yuchnoye zhivotnoye* (beast of burden).

It's 10:00 p.m. and the end of the third tent approaches. There's a buzz in the air as folks around me can now see the end of the queue. Behind me song breaks out. At first just a few people pick up the tune, but soon the entire tent is singing "Ukraine Has Not Yet Perished," their national anthem. It's loud and passionate—like an emotional dam breaking as the sound moves through the tent. Later, I translate the short chorus and verse:

> The glory and freedom of Ukraine has not yet perished
> Luck will still smile on us brother-Ukrainians.

Our enemies will die, as the dew does in the sunshine,
and we, too, brothers, we'll live happily in our land.
We'll not spare either our souls or bodies to get freedom
and we'll prove that we brothers are of Kozak kin.

Again, we stop for about thirty minutes with no movement. We are very close now. Ahead, the line, which has been about five people across, contracts as railings on either side of the crowd narrow the people into two queues. The female Ukrainian soldier in charge is letting groups of about thirty at a time enter the lines. Those people then wait until a second soldier appears from a side door and instructs the next group to enter through the double doors.

Zip trots toward the doors and sits. It's the first time I've seen the dog stop moving. The Ukrainian soldier walks over and tousles Zip's ears. The dog nuzzles her leg; they clearly know each other. It brings me comfort to know that Zip is accounted for.

At 10:45 p.m. my group enters the building in two lines. Inside there are six windows, two of which are manned by Ukrainian immigration officers. It's my turn and I hand the officer my passport. She flips through the pages and stops on a stamp from Panama dated July 2019. Fortunately, Panama has condemned Russia's invasion, so a second later she stamps my passport. Again, no questions asked and I'm through. It has taken me eight and a half hours to travel six hundred feet (about 180 meters), at a rate of about seventy feet per hour. It's 11:00 p.m. as I leave the Ukrainian immigration building and walk through the Grey Zone back toward Poland.

While the queue on the Ukrainian side of the border is long, the fact that only a few people clear customs every ten to fifteen minutes means there's just a slow, steady trickle arriving to Polish immigration. I get in line with about twenty others, and unlike at the Ukrainian office I've just exited, there's an X-ray machine here where bags are scanned. I meet an aid worker named Paul from Manchester, England, who volunteered after he saw the images from the maternity hospital that was bombed in Mariupol on March 9, 2022. A telecommunications worker, Paul asked his boss for three weeks off to volunteer in Poland. "When he said no, I quit." The next day, his boss called him and asked if he was serious. When Paul told him he was, his boss approved the time off.

"Do you see that knife?" Paul says, pointing to the ground on the other side of the thick fence. A steak knife lies in the dirt. "The women toss their knives there. Last week there was a pile of about four hundred knives that we cleared away."

Here, just steps away from Poland, Ukrainian women feel safe enough to dispose of weapons they've carried on their journeys. I hear from an Israeli organization that many women ask for rape kits, but the organization is out of them right now. Some mothers need them for their children.

I clear Polish immigration at 11:36 p.m. and walk back to the humanitarian corridor in Medyka. Throughout my nine-hour crossing I've been updating Stasz, who has been helping the staff at the Operation Blessing tent. He and I exit the humanitarian corridor, walk the short distance to our car, and drive back to our hostel in nearby Przemyśl without saying much. It has been a day beyond words.

CHAPTER 6

Exploited

It's hard to imagine enduring more trauma than a person living in the center of a life-threatening military conflict. Yet at the border crossings of the war in Ukraine, after women and children seeking refuge across the border spend weeks living in basements, enduring air raids and missile strikes, and oftentimes leaving loved ones behind, another danger awaits them: the specter of sex traffickers.

Particularly vulnerable are young, single Ukrainian women who are headed for—or have just crossed—the border into the neighboring nations of Romania, Moldova, Hungary, Slovakia, Poland, Belarus, and Russia. For many Ukrainians who make the crossing at Medyka—the busiest transit point for Ukraine's refugees—the nearby Polish town of Przemyśl is their jumping-off point to destinations farther into Europe. Some have relatives awaiting them, while others have no one. Particularly vulnerable are the women who have no set address toward which they are traveling. Often alone, they are targeted by sex traffickers who have descended on the border towns of neighboring nations.

These traffickers pose as transit hosts or employment recruiters who offer rooms, meals, and the promise of jobs across Europe. Instead, the women they engage with are entrapped and trafficked in the illicit sex trade.

At the borders in Poland, I was made particularly aware of the sex trafficking abuses taking place there. I connected with Alejandro DeHoyos, an Emmy Award–winning filmmaker from San Antonio, Texas, who spent several weeks in eastern Poland and western Ukraine capturing footage for an upcoming series called *Passport Pastors*. He had been interacting with two nonprofit organizations: Awakening Europe and an American group called Solid Rock Mission, which has a strong presence in Ukraine.

These two groups are working together to answer refugees' logistical questions, to distribute sex trafficking awareness pamphlets, and to offer encouragement and prayer. Each day, these groups' workers head out to the train and bus stations on both sides of the border. They also ride the trains and buses and spend time with people in a more relaxed setting than the bustle of a busy border crossing. And when they see potential sex traffickers, they report them to the local police. In late March 2022 they claim to have given tips that led to the interrogation of dozens of alleged sex traffickers.

In one situation, Alejandro tells me, several people from AE were in Lviv, near the train station, chatting with a woman from Ukraine. At the end of their conversation they exchanged numbers so they could keep in touch. A few days later the woman reached out to one of the women on the AE team and said she had boarded a large bus carrying only young Ukrainian women to the Polish border. The men in charge, she said, were not taking them where they said they would go, and the woman was alarmed. She gave the bus's location to AE, and in turn, the authorities were notified.

The police were able to track down the bus and apprehend the alleged sex traffickers. As a result thirty women were now free and able to continue their journeys in safety. If not for one assertive refugee, and a handful of concerned volunteers, these women would most likely have ended up in a very bad place.

Alejandro describes a direct run-in that he had with traffickers. It was a cold, rainy day in early April on the Ukrainian side of the border. He and other volunteers were working on the street where cars and buses line up waiting to clear customs. One of the female volunteers was approached by a man who emerged from the side of a building. He asked her if she needed a ride or if she had a boyfriend. It felt ominous, and she sensed danger. When she told the middle-aged man she was fine, he moved closer to her in a threatening way.

She quickly left and made her way back across the street to Alejandro and told him the story. They spotted the man, who had walked over to a blue truck and was standing beside the driver's side door, talking with the driver. There was a female child sitting in the middle seat. She looked afraid and sad. Alejandro took photos of the man and the truck, and he and the aid worker left to find the authorities. Ukrainian border patrol told him to report the incident to the police, which he did. By the time they all arrived on the scene, however, the blue truck was gone. "It still haunts me," Alejandro confides, "seeing that young girl sitting there with those two strange-looking men."

In a third incident, Alejandro and some yellow-vested colleagues came across a minibus carrying twelve young women, along with a middle-aged driver and a middle-aged woman. His group chatted through the bus window with one of the girls, who said they were dancers. But something felt off, as if the answer was rehearsed or forced. Not wanting to miss another chance to help someone in possible danger, Alejandro called ahead to the Polish border police, and sent them photos of the driver, the van, and the license plate. Polish police assured him that they would flag the van and investigate any potential wrongdoing.

Another group working tirelessly at the Ukraine-Poland border is Unbound Now, an international anti-human-trafficking organization based in Texas. Amanda Buenger, J.D., executive director of Unbound Bryan College Station, gave this report on the organization's website upon her return:

> During our trip, myself and teammate Detective Joseph Scaramucci [a nationally renowned law enforcement expert on human trafficking] felt led to walk down a particular street in Ukraine. This area was clearly a transportation hub and was filled with Ukrainians getting in and out of buses, vans, and other vehicles. Refugees figuring out how to get across the border without knowledge of how the process works are most vulnerable to the tactics of exploiters. These transition points are places we know bad actors target people in need.
>
> As we walked down the street observing our surroundings, something didn't feel right. We walked by a put-together woman who was talking with three women and asking for their travel documents, including their passport information. We approached these women and with the help of our translator, began to ask them about the context of the conversation. They shared that they had been promised transportation over the border and connection to a driver in Poland in exchange for a fee and agreeing to carry a bag across with them. They had given the woman their passports and paid already.
>
> We immediately pulled the three women aside and indicated that this was a trafficking situation. The woman had lied to them about the cost to cross to the border; there is no fee. She lied about needing their travel documents; only the border agents need to see them. She lied about having a verified driver; only certain drivers who are registered with proper documentation can pick people up on the other side.
>
> We walked with these women to the line to cross the border, continuing to tell them not to trust this woman and what she was saying. Shortly thereafter, the woman trafficker became frustrated, realizing we had intercepted the attempt, and she

ran off. We were able to get pictures and run some history on this particular individual which confirmed her involvement with the human trafficking world.[1]

Unfortunately, these stories are not rare—and people in war zones are particularly vulnerable to sex traffickers. Desperation, disorientation, and exhaustion combine to make refugees affected by war and disaster particularly vulnerable prey for the ruthless people profiting from human misery.

Human trafficking is the fastest-growing criminal industry in the world, with more than forty million victims worldwide.[2] And it's happening today—in our communities. In other words, while refugees in combat zones like Ukraine, Syria, Yemen, South Sudan, and the Congo are arguably the most vulnerable, the human trafficking trade is ubiquitous.

Equally disturbing are reports that many Ukrainians are being forcibly sent to Russia. In hot spots like Mariupol, locals are sometimes sent to "filtration camps" before being forcibly relocated across the Russian border. Numbers are hard to come by, but of the one million Ukrainians who had arrived in Russia by mid-May,[3] Ukraine's President Zelensky says that "hundreds of thousands" of them have been deported against their will.[4]

U.S. Ambassador to the United Nations Linda Thomas-Greenfield said, "I do not need to spell out what these so-called 'filtration camps' are reminiscent of. It's chilling and we cannot look away." She cited credible reports—including from the Mariupol City Council—that Russian Federal Security Service (FSB) agents have been confiscating passports, IDs, and cell phones, and separating Ukrainian families from each other.[5] And some refugees—including orphaned children—are being relocated to places as far away as Sakhalin Island just north of Japan, some seven thousand kilometers from Ukraine.[6]

Among the criminally active along Ukraine's borders there are thousands of others who are fighting to protect the same vulnerable women and children. Organizations like Awakening Europe and Unbound Now are working hard on the ground, as are groups such as Exodus Cry, a U.S.-based anti-sex-trafficking organization, the Global Alliance Against Traffic in Women (GAATW), and UNICEF, among many others.

There is hope for Ukraine's uprooted and displaced, and we all play a part in becoming informed and active in the fight against human- and sex-trafficking activity. Pray. Advocate. Give of your time, treasure, and talents.

To learn how to fight human trafficking, see the "Resources" section at the end of the book.

CHAPTER 7

Johnny and Ira

I t's an international romance straight out of a movie: A Canadian boy with Ukrainian roots goes to summer camp and meets a Ukrainian girl. They are just friends—even though every camp photo shows them standing next to each other. Over the next several years, the Canadian boy grows into a man and travels to Ukraine to work with orphans. While there, he crosses paths with the Ukrainian girl, who is now a young woman of nineteen. They fall in love. She visits him in Canada, and he visits her in Lviv, her hometown. A marriage proposal is made and accepted. The Semeniuks both get jobs at a prestigious American school in the beautiful capital city of Kyiv and begin their lives together as man and wife.

Ira Semeniuk describes their life as newlyweds living and working in one of Europe's most beautiful capitals in 2009: "We would work all week at the school, and then Friday night we would board a hot Ukrainian train and travel overnight to the eastern city of Kryvyy Rih" (a large industrial town about four hundred kilometers southeast of Kyiv). She continues, "We'd arrive at 6:00 a.m., grab breakfast at McDonald's, and then spend our Saturday working with orphans and people with disabilities, before boarding the 9:00 p.m. overnight train back to Kyiv in time to make Sunday morning church service."

The two of them smile as I sit with them at a lovely café in the picturesque town of Bochnia, Poland, tucked in the hills about thirty-five kilometers southwest of Krakow. "We did that for five years, until our son was born," Ira adds.

The couple's flat was on the western side of Kyiv when the Revolution of Dignity began in November 2013. They witnessed firsthand Ukraine's struggle to shrug off the political and ideological restraints of an increasingly repressive Russian oligarchy. They could see some of the violence outside their window. At one point, they responded by lending a hand to injured protesters during Euromaidan, the protests between Western-leaning Ukrainians and the pro-Russian regime of President Viktor Yanukovych that turned deadly in late January and February 2014.

"It was intense, and we would just pray every day and trust that the violence wouldn't escalate," adds Johnny, remembering how Ira was pregnant with their first son, Levi, at the time. (Their second son, Luka, was born in October 2021.)

"My two sons were both born into intense conflicts," adds Ira.

On February 21, 2014, the Ukrainian parliament voted overwhelmingly for the removal of President Viktor Yanukovych and for the creation of a new government. It was a buoyant time in Kyiv, but the excitement was short-lived. In March 2014 pro-Russian factions in the eastern districts of Donetsk and Luhansk—bolstered by heavy Russian support—began an armed civil war. Around the same time, Putin's "little green men" (Russian soldiers dressed in unmarked uniforms) annexed Crimea. Johnny is quick to point out that the invasion of Ukraine did not start on February 24, 2022, but almost exactly eight years earlier in the Donbas region. "For Ukrainians, the recent invasion is just the most recent attack on their country," he notes.

The Semeniuks had come to Lviv a week before the invasion, as the U.S. Embassy in Kyiv had told workers at the American school to shut it down and evacuate. The Semeniuks couldn't leave Ukraine by air because Johnny had COVID-19. Instead, they went to stay with Ira's mom and brother, Yuri, who live in Lviv. Like many Kyivans, they assumed that Lviv—some four hundred kilometers west—would be safe in the event that an invasion actually occurred.

The couple expected to be in Lviv for just a couple of weeks. "We figured that things would die down, and then we could return to our home in Kyiv," says Johnny. Early on the morning of February 24 Johnny and Ira awoke to air raid sirens and a string of texts from Johnny's relatives in Canada. "They told us the Russian army had started their invasion," he says.

"All day on the twenty-fourth we were debating what to do and realized it was best to go," Ira says. "We didn't want to leave my mom, but she refused to leave her home. Even though I knew my brother was staying and would look after her, it was very difficult."

That night Johnny, Ira, and their two young boys left Lviv in their Volkswagen SUV. The seventy-five-kilometer drive to the Polish border—which normally takes less than two hours—took them an entire day. Johnny adds, "We said good-bye that night not knowing if we would see Ira's family again. We crossed the border into Poland about twenty-five hours later."

In doing so, the Semeniuk family can now be counted among the nearly 3.5 million Ukrainian residents who have fled the war into Poland. After air strikes around Lviv turned deadly in mid-April, Ira was finally able to convince her mom to join them in Poland. But her brother, his wife, and their three children remain in Lviv.

Once settled in Bochnia, Johnny and Ira jumped into action, looking for ways to help their Ukrainian brothers and sisters. In fact, when Johnny was searching for housing in Poland, he purposefully chose Bochnia for its easy access to the border and close proximity to Krakow, a major staging area for international humanitarian aid shipments.

"We were in constant contact with people all over Ukraine, and requests were flooding in from towns like Bucha, Irpin, Chernihiv, and Kharkiv—some of the hardest-hit cities," Johnny says. One of the things the Semeniuks prayed about was how to offer the most practical help. They were teachers, not aid workers. But they knew that the needs were great. As well, the large humanitarian organizations were taking care of a lot of the most basic demands, such as food and water. However, what about things like insulin for diabetics, statin for those suffering from high cholesterol, anti-stroke drugs, antibiotics, or other everyday—but critical—medications, especially for the elderly?

Johnny made the rounds to all the pharmacies in Bochnia, pleading for as many drugs as he could purchase. "I definitely wore out my welcome with some of the pharmacists!" he jokes. Ira went to work through social media to raise money to pay for the medicines. It was the definition of a grassroots effort.

What Johnny, Ira, and their friends needed now was a consistent way to get the supplies into Ukraine, so the couple prayed that God would open the doors for their transportation needs. A day or so later Johnny was at a radio store, trying to bridge the language barrier with the clerk. A man nearby who spoke both Polish and English offered to translate. It turns out that Robert, who is American, was interested in helping out as well.

"I called Robert a couple of days later, after receiving a request for thermal blankets," says Johnny. "He picked me up in his Ford F150—a rare sight in Poland—and took me around Krakow, buying tons of food and supplies." Since then, Robert has connected the Semeniuks with many key contacts. He owns a building company and has connections with drivers who are part of the International Police Association, whose members have special licenses to take goods into Ukraine, such as supplies and armor (and of course, humanitarian goods).

When they first started to collect and deliver aid, Johnny, Ira, and their friends used a couple of converted vans and filled them with medicine, tourniquets, medical gauze, thermal sighting scopes, thermal blankets, body armor, food, water, and other critical supplies. They would meet drivers of large commercial buses at a McDonald's around midnight, right inside the Polish border. They'd load up the buses with their donations as the drivers prepared to head back into Ukraine after dropping off refugees in Poland.

The vicissitudes of war led to certain doors closing while others opened. For a while the couple was able to transport aid items to the Medyka border crossing and drive into the Grey Zone (the area between both borders). They unloaded the vans and placed the supplies on the buses there. It was a win-win as the buses were virtually empty, and the bus drivers were heading back to Lviv in any case. In Lviv the goods were once again unloaded, this time at a distribution center, and from there, drivers from various cities across Ukraine made perilous journeys back to the frontline cities hit the hardest.

Recently, however, the rules changed again and the Semeniuks had to pivot. Johnny says, "I brought stuff in myself this past week and gave it to Ira's brother just inside Ukraine, at a different crossing point. Then we also have had my cousin come to Bochnia all the way from the Kyiv region with a huge van. We moved more than three tons of aid over several trips as well. Essentially, we use whatever means we can and adapt as we need to."

To date, the Semeniuks and faithful friends—Ukrainians, Poles, Americans, Canadians, among others—have raised more than $70,000 and have transported more than twenty van loads of goods across the border into Ukraine.

I ask the couple what people back in the United States, Canada, and other concerned nations can do to help the Ukrainians in their life-and-death struggle.

"Pray for the end of the war, first of all," says Ira, her piercing blue eyes intense and filled with emotion. "Second, pray that God would direct you to the organization that He puts on your heart—and then give. And give again."

"The demand far outpaces the supply," adds Johnny. "I know it's hard when you are far away from a conflict zone like Ukraine, but people need to know that every penny they give is critical."

Ira adds, "One of my high school students connected online and shared her disappointment with me that she could not give more money. But I told her that her forty-five-dollar donation would buy two much-needed tourniquets for wounded soldiers. So for less than fifty dollars her donation could save two lives."

Amazingly, between attending to his family and working with Ira and others to organize their supply runs to the border, Johnny continues to teach online. Despite the war, many students at their international school are still attending classes. "We really never stopped teaching, because COVID-19 had already helped us transition to an online teaching model," says Johnny. His students are now scattered across the globe, but many are still joining online from inside Ukraine.

As long as there is need, Johnny and Ira will continue to raise funds, gather supplies, and make their runs to the border. "What else would we do?" adds Ira, her eyes pooling with tears. "My country is on fire. Loved ones—including old people and children—are dying. To turn away would be to reject the heart of God for the people."

To give to the Semeniuks' aid efforts, and for a list of additional aid organizations, see the "Resources" section at the back of the book.

CHAPTER 8

Esther's Heritage

Esther is the only book in the Bible that does not mention God by name.

It tells the incredible story of a Hebrew girl who gains favor with a Persian king in whose kingdom her people are enslaved. Despite dark plots against her people, she prevails, saves the Hebrews from genocide, and ascends the throne. It's a powerful example of how God's presence is the essence of how He works through women and men—even when His name isn't mentioned.

When it was time to capture the story of Esther Fedorkevich, my co-laborer in this book project, I encouraged Esther to write her story herself. She demurred and said, "You're the writer and I'm the agent and marketer. Go interview my parents!" In the end, that approach worked out because for one of the most gifted entrepreneurs I've ever worked with, Esther is fairly shy when it comes to talking about herself.

I have no problem telling Esther's story, because in its pages are the fingerprints of a God who has raised up a Ukrainian family—actually, two Ukrainian families—for such a time as this. And like the Old Testament's Queen Esther, I believe God is using her namesake, my colleague Esther, in strategic ways during a troubling and historic time.

But I'm getting ahead of myself. Let's start at the beginning.

Esther is the oldest daughter in a family of seven kids, including three older brothers, a younger sister, and two younger brothers. Her father, Paul Chodniewicz, was born in Buenos Aires, Argentina, where his Ukrainian parents emigrated in 1928. At that time, Argentina would cover travel costs for European families looking for fresh opportunities, and the Chodniewicz family answered the call. Paul's parents spoke Ukrainian to him growing up, but he didn't want anything to do with it. "I would tell them I was a proud Argentine boy who only spoke Spanish," he says.

When Paul was sixteen his family moved to the United States, seeking a better life. Though leaving Argentina was difficult, Paul soon became active in a Ukrainian Assembly of God church in Newark, New Jersey, which later moved to the town of Union. Paul and other young men in the church formed a musical group, with Paul on vocals and guitar. Soon after, the gospel group began to travel North America ministering in churches or other venues.

In 1973 the group made their first trip to Ukraine. "A lot of Ukrainians would come and the older ladies would sit down front. I noticed they all wore colorful headscarves, just as my mom did every day of her life. And their hands looked like my mom's hands," he recalls. "I thought, *O God, these are my people!* The Holy Spirit made a life-changing connection for me and I was no longer Argentine—though I love Argentina—but Ukrainian." In spite of his earlier boyhood objections, Paul was now able to speak and understand Ukrainian because of his parents.

Not long after Paul's parents left Ukraine for Argentina, Nina's grandparents fled Ukraine to escape religious persecution and severe famine. In 1932 Josef Stalin seized Ukraine's grain supply in response to rising Ukrainian nationalism. Called the Holodomor, this man-made famine led to the starvation and death of nearly four million Ukrainians between 1932 and 1933. Ninety years later, it's chilling to see Russian troops once again confiscating shipments of Ukrainian grain.

"In the early 1930s my grandparents walked into China, searching for freedom and a better life," Nina says. "It would take thirty years for my family to find it." That opportunity came when Nina was six, and her family emigrated to Australia. "In those days you traveled to Hong Kong to wait for the next available ship, no matter where it was going. In our case the ship was headed to Australia," she says. When she was sixteen, the family moved once again, this time to Vancouver, Canada.

On a ministry trip to Vancouver in 1970 a young Christian singer and his group performed at a small church where Nina's family was involved. Paul and Nina met and quickly fell in love. Five months later they married and set up their home in New Jersey. Paul adds, "My mother always told me that if the parents are good people, the daughter will be, too. And my mom was right!" On May 16, 2022, the couple celebrated their fifty-first wedding anniversary.

Paul's first trip to Ukraine in 1973 was during the Soviet Union's ascension. "We brought Bibles and music records to give away, but the border guards wanted to confiscate them, including our personal Bibles. We fought the guards about it for twelve hours and told them to look at the pages to see our notes and highlights. Eventually they let us take a few Bibles and records in. We later found out that the soldiers turned around and sold what they did confiscate from us—which is fine because the Word of God still got out," Paul says.

During Paul's first trip to Ukraine with the music group after the dissolution of the USSR in the early 1990s, he says people would run to the front to accept Jesus. "Things had just opened up, and there was an intense hunger for God. People cried and kissed their Bibles as we passed them out, because many had never owned their own Bible." His co-laborer over the years has been George Davidiuk, the beloved Ukrainian-American evangelist who is widely known in Ukraine.

Meanwhile, back in New Jersey the Chodniewicz family was growing as Nina managed their busy household and Paul built a successful contracting business. They tell me that their young daughter Esther was scrappy, tenacious, and athletic. Nina adds, "She was tough and prided herself on being able to do anything her older brothers could do."

By high school Esther had convinced her dad to help her rent a sales cart in a nearby mall to sell gift items. These are the kinds of small kiosks that sell sunglasses or bath salts extracted from the Dead Sea. Over two summers Esther built a thriving business and was able to make a tidy sum. On the basketball court, she was a gifted McDonald's All-American shooting guard who was offered a scholarship to play at the University of Southern California.

But something happened that disrupted her dreams of basketball stardom: Esther fell in love with a boy from church named Jimmy Fedorkevich—a first-generation Ukrainian musician and worship leader. Rather than accept the basketball scholarship, she worked to help put Jimmy through the prestigious Berkeley School of Music. She says there was a higher goal: to see God glorified in her marriage and through her husband's worship ministry. One week after the couple married, they moved to Nashville, where Jimmy accepted a position as lead worship pastor at Christ Church Nashville, a thriving evangelical congregation.

"I don't have any regrets—I was nineteen and Jimmy and I had this mutual passion to see Jesus glorified through music," Esther says. When the two of them were growing up, both the Chodniewicz and Fedorkevich families took their kids to church several times a week, immersing them in the large Ukrainian community in the greater New Jersey area.

Esther echoes her parents' love and commitment to Ukraine. Indeed, the *zholud* (acorn) didn't fall far from the tree, because in Esther one sees a mix of her parents' giftings: a heart for the lost and suffering, and a masterful business mind to "do stuff for the Kingdom of God." And that's what Esther did, taking a job with internationally renowned financial advisor and bestselling author Dave Ramsey, where she cut her teeth in marketing and publishing.

After another short stint with a Nashville publishing house, Esther decided to launch out on her own as a literary agent. "My main goal was to find great books that have transformative messages," she said. "I knew God wanted me to find those voices that did not yet have a voice, and get them published."

In her first year as an agent she made $12,000, but she knew God doesn't despise small beginnings, so she stuck with it. She found her first clients in the youth departments of large churches and at youth ministry conventions. Two of those leaders were John Bevere and Steve Furtick. That strategy was a sound one, as both have gone on to become bestselling authors.

"Growing up with five brothers was awesome preparation for being a female agent in a male Christian publishing culture," she says. At that time—in the early 2000s—there were only a handful of women in executive leadership positions in faith-based publishing. "I wasn't intimidated by anyone because my brothers had always treated me like a guy," she quips. Slowly but surely, she adds, she has seen progress for women in the publishing world.

It was at this time in her agency's early days that I met Esther. She represented research expert and bestselling author George Barna, and I served as George's publisher at Regal Books. She was confident but not arrogant, with a light touch and a natural, unforced way with people.

By 2003 Esther and Jimmy had started a family, and it was fun to see the Fedorkevichs thriving so well in Tennessee. A daughter, Lexi, and a son, Paul, made things complete. Over the next several years our paths crossed at conventions, and I updated her on my family's journey.

Esther reached out and said she was praying for my wife, Suzanne, when she was diagnosed with breast cancer in 2007. (Suzanne is now fifteen years cancer-free.) And she took a genuine interest in our journey to adopt our son from Ukraine, which happened at the same time. Of course, as a full-blooded Ukrainian she loved the idea and prayed us through that experience as well.

Eventually life took the Fedorkevich family to Austin, Texas, where they live today. When a job I'd taken right before the pandemic didn't work out, Esther called me the next business day and offered me a position. "I want to hire you," she said, in her typically blunt but winsome style.

I accepted her offer. As writer-in-residence for the Fedd Agency, I saw firsthand how Esther is gifted at recognizing a person's gifts, leveraging them, and then getting out of the way.

Just recently one of her clients' titles became the agency's ninetieth book to reach the *New York Times* bestseller list—an incredible feat. And while Esther has grown the Fedd Agency into a highly successful business, her first priority has remained fixed on God. She gives a nod to her parents in this regard. "I watched my parents go through a lot of ups and downs, and they never lost their focus for Jesus," she says.

When Esther was just fourteen, her dad was diagnosed with colon cancer. While the doctors gave a grim prognosis, she remembers her dad telling her that Jesus was going to heal him. Six months later, her dad's oncologist brought amazing news: The latest blood tests had revealed zero cancer cells. Her dad had been right. "That was such a faith builder for me," says Esther.

Paul and Nina are quick to say that during Paul's cancer journey, they lost their business and eventually had to start again from scratch. Eventually they were able to get back on their feet, but it made a lasting impression. "We don't hold on to material things," Paul says. "Life's experiences are temporary, and we try to encourage our children that money is fine, but it can be gone in a second. The only thing that endures is what we do for Christ."

Esther received the message. When I first approached her with the idea for this book, she immediately embraced it. In short order she secured a contract deal with Dwight Baker, the president of Baker Publishing Group, and told him that she would donate all her proceeds to aid those affected by the war in Ukraine.

"The goal is to give voice to the people of Ukraine—to tell their stories," Esther says.

It's what her parents have been doing for more than fifty years—helping shine the light of God's love on the country of their ancestors. Over the past half century Paul has made thirty-plus trips to Ukraine, and in that time has come to know the spiritual climate there very well. "We had to acquire special religious visas to enter the USSR, and we would spend up to a month in Ukraine. When you were there you could feel the oppression of the communist system," he says. "It was this sense of darkness and fear. It is the same spirit you see today with this invasion—it is evil, but God is on the throne."

Both Paul and Nina have family histories that span the rise and fall of the Soviet Union. They experienced firsthand the sociopolitical and spiritual *glasnost* that swept the former Soviet republics after the fall of the Berlin Wall. They have traveled throughout Ukraine and stayed in friends' homes, and they watched in horror as events began to unfold on February 24, 2022. As the war rages on, they laugh and cry with Ukrainians over Zoom from bombed-out cities, and pray with parents whose sons are fighting on the front lines.

Though—like Esther—Nina isn't big on talking about herself, it's obvious she's a prayer warrior. Our phone conversations are about the needs of Ukrainians and the effects of Russia's invasion, and how we can all do more to help. She is a tireless advocate for those suffering in war-torn Ukraine.

"We have hundreds of friends from all across Ukraine, and God is at work in a mighty way despite the terrible carnage and senseless killing going on," Nina tells me. She and Paul are in constant contact with people on the ground there, and meeting needs where they can.

As I planned to head to Poland and Ukraine to research stories for this book, Nina connected me with their daughter-in-law's brother, Johnny Semeniuk, and his wife, Ira, whose story you read in the previous chapter. As I mentioned there, they fled Ukraine and are now moving tons of humanitarian aid into the country from their temporary home near Krakow, Poland. I was privileged to share two meals with the Semeniuks while in Poland, and to hear firsthand the tangible ways they are acting as God's hands and feet in Ukraine.

As well, Nina has a pragmatic, singular mindset about the war in Ukraine. From her living room in New Jersey, she operates a grassroots prayer chain to "war in the heavenlies" for her country of heritage.

Though their hearts break for friends and loved ones suffering from the war, Paul and Nina's prayer is that Ukraine would experience revival in the midst of the brokenness. Paul adds, "In spite of the horrible things that are happening, and no matter how dark it gets, Jesus will prevail in Ukraine."

That is a sentiment that father, mother, and daughter all embrace.

CHAPTER 9

Maksym and Roksolana

For Ukrainians, February 24, 2022, is a date that will go down in infamy—similar to December 7, 1941, for Americans, and September 11, 2001.

It was an infamous day for Maksym and Roksolana (not their real names). It was the day the war came to their doorstep.

About six weeks after the start of Russia's illegal invasion of Ukraine, I am sitting in a pleasant apartment outside Krakow, eating pizza with Maksym and Roksolana, along with other friends. The couple are young professionals who work with Johnny, Ira, and colleague Gale Stubbs at the American school in Kyiv (see "Johnny and Ira," chapter 7). Their two-year-old daughter, Myroslava, sleeps in a nearby room as we eat and chat.

The mood in the room grows somber as pizza boxes are cleared and the couple begin to tell their story. Unlike the Semeniuks, who evacuated Kyiv before the war broke out, Maksym and Roksolana decided to stay to see how things would play out. In the weeks leading up to the invasion, they had been listening to President Joe Biden's warnings of an imminent attack. But like many Ukrainians, they weren't convinced that Putin would actually send in troops. Also, they had their young daughter to consider. She was just days away from surgery to correct a heart valve defect, and the couple wanted to see it through.

When the invasion did begin, the couple was torn. But everything had changed now, and the surgery had been postponed indefinitely with the invasion now a reality. It was time to leave Kyiv. Maksym's mother and father lived in a village called Motyzhyn, which is about forty kilometers west of the capital. It is a quiet, out-of-the-way place holding no strategic military importance, so they assumed they would be safe there.

February 24 was an intense, chaotic day in Kyiv, as many residents had the same idea as the couple. The usual twenty-minute drive to the edge of the city now took six hours as cars jammed the main routes out of the capital. While Roksolana had been prepared and had packed everyone's bags two weeks before, she had forgotten one thing: the family's passports.

"We need to go back!" she exclaimed to Maksym as their car inched closer to exiting the city. So they swung around and were now battling the traffic in the opposite direction. Eventually they determined it would be faster for Roksolana to walk the rest of the way to their flat, so she got out of the car and started back on foot.

"It was so crazy because people were out walking their dogs as if nothing unusual were happening. Joggers in full work-out gear were taking leisurely runs, as if a major army weren't marching toward the city," Roksolana adds. "It was so cold and I was terrified and kept looking at the sky, wondering when the bombs might start dropping."

Passports sorted, the family left the city for the countryside. All was quiet once they cleared traffic out of Kyiv, and they arrived in the peaceful village of Motyzhyn. Maksym's father had had to have his leg amputated two months before, so he was still recovering in a wheelchair.

What the family did not know was that the Russian army had chosen the roads through the village as their main route in their efforts to encircle Kyiv. Rather than escaping into a sleepy village to wait out the fighting, the family was now directly in the path of the Russian advance.

Maksym describes life in a war zone: "On the first night, we slept upstairs—but we could not sleep. And then on the second day I moved my wife and daughter to the basement. But we could not move my dad, so he slept on the first floor of the house. During the day we remained very quiet as we saw tanks roll through the village, about three hundred meters away. They were getting closer."

Word came through that some neighbors had been shot because they had peeked out their window and someone in a tank had seen them. Why that particular house? No one knew—a random killing. The head of the town, Olha Sukhenko, was executed, along with her husband, Ihor, their twenty-five-year-old son, Oleksandr, and another village resident, their bodies found in shallow graves in a nearby grove of pine trees.

The tanks and shooting grew closer. Around the third day, the household lost electricity and water, and they had to get their water from a nearby pump. They had three power banks, which they used to keep one phone charged at all times. That day is when they heard tanks roll by the house, some just outside the window. Many were flying the red flag of the Soviet Union. At night Maksym would make his way up to the roof of the two-story home and fix Russian positions using Google Maps. Once marked, he would use a secure portal on his phone to alert local Ukrainian forces.

During the day, the sounds of artillery and small arms fire were constant. Grad rockets started landing in the village on day four, and they could see four neighbors' houses in flames. The fighting intensified due to Ukrainian army resistance. The Ukrainians were having great success destroying Russian tanks in the area using Turkish Bayraktar TB2 drones and other anti-tank weapons.

"We heard the explosions, and we could see the wreckage of the Russian tanks," says Maksym.

He and Roksolana prayed that God would show them the right time to leave. Maksym knew he had to get his family out, along with his elderly parents. Their car was low on gasoline, but thankfully they had set aside fuel before the war, which they had been using to run a generator to produce electricity for the house.

Maksym says, "I knew it was only a matter of time before the soldiers either bombed our house or decided to raid it." One afternoon the family packed all the belongings they could, removing Myroslava's car seat and any other extra items to make room for Maksym's parents and his dad's wheelchair. Around 2:00 p.m. they called a contact in the village to the west to see if the route was safe. The woman said it was not. They then called the police, who verified that the way west was unsafe.

"It was a very emotional, tense time," says Roksolana. "The timing of our departure really became a life-and-death decision." And despite the two negative reports regarding the dangers of their escape route, they decided the time was now. "I can't explain it—it was as though God gave my husband this strong impression to go *now*," adds Roksolana.

Moving as quickly as they could, Maksym carried his dad and helped him into the back seat, and stored his wheelchair in the trunk. They then loaded up the family with only a few possessions placed on their laps, and headed out shortly after 2:00 p.m.

In an ingenious move to disorient the Russians, locals throughout the region had removed many of the street signs to make it more difficult for the enemy to navigate. The problem was that as Maksym drove he could not depend on road signs. As well, GPS was disabled in the region to make it that much more difficult for the Russians to maneuver.

Maksym was driving very slowly, because he did not know what dangers might lie ahead. In the distance Roksolana spotted a large black object in the center of the road. Was it a Russian tank or a Ukrainian tank? As they inched closer to the object, they could make out that it was a destroyed Russian tank. "After that," says Maksym, "I floored it and sped out of there as fast as I could. My other fear was that the debris in the road would cut my tires."

He drove down streets littered with blown-up tanks and bullet-riddled cars strewn across the road. As they moved west they came across Ukrainian roadblocks. At each new checkpoint they asked if the way ahead were safe; each time the army told them they could not confirm the road's safety.

Roksolana says, "We saw a car on the left side, and we decided to ask them if we were headed in the right direction. But now I understand that it didn't make sense—why would any car stop in such a dangerous place at that moment? We could see that the car had just been shot up. Everyone had been shot."

The farther west they drove, however, the safer they felt. "I was praying the whole time, asking God to direct my husband and to make a path for us to safety," says Roksolana. "And we did make it."

Maksym says, "The hardest thing was that I had to leave my parents' dog. With my father's wheelchair in the trunk and five of us in our small car packed with luggage, there just wasn't any room." His voice catching, he adds, "I left a big bag of dog food and a lot of water for him." A neighbor has been looking after the dog, and the family is hopeful for a reunion.

The family headed toward Lviv and the relative safety of western Ukraine. But then, just a few kilometers outside Lviv, Maksym's dad suffered a stroke. They were able to call the paramedics, who arrived within several minutes.

"If my dad had suffered a stroke back in Motyzhyn, there would have been no help for him there," Maksym says. A hospital in Lviv was able to stabilize his dad—and most likely saved his life.

Meanwhile, across the border in Poland, friends Johnny and Ira Semeniuk had found an apartment in Bochnia, just outside Krakow. They spoke to the building's landlord, who told them that the apartment next to theirs was also vacant. The landlord even said that she would reduce the rent for Maksym and Roksolana. Through the help of their friends, the family was actually able to move in rent-free.

Roksolana smiles and says, "The fact that Maksym's dad had a medical emergency only after leaving the war zone, and just minutes away from the best hospital in the region—that is amazing." As well, she says, they were able to meet with the finest cardiologists in Krakow, and their daughter's heart procedure was performed successfully in late May.

"When I look back," say Roksolana, eyes shining, "I clearly see the hand of God. He guided my husband and told him the perfect time to leave the basement. He guided our car down shattered roads full of metal and destruction, and showed us the way out."

She pauses, grabs Maksym's hand, and adds, "I believe our journey has been a miracle. We are so thankful to God."

Postscript: A few weeks after I met Roksolana, she emailed me an update. Once the Ukrainians recaptured the village of Motyzhyn, neighbors were able to check on the house. She wrote, "Now we know for sure that Russians were in the house in Motyzhyn. They had been looking for money and had destroyed many things. So I assume if we wouldn't have left, I wouldn't have been able to email you now."

Roksolana notes that on May 12, 2022, the *Wall Street Journal* shared their own investigation about the Motyzhyn area.[1] She says, "Many people in cars were shot on the same day we left, but two and a half hours later." The road they used to leave the city—now called the Road of Death—was the scene of multiple civilian deaths and atrocities.

CHAPTER 10

The Vest

On March 5, just outside Kyiv on the outskirts of Bucha, a British *Sky News* team of five came under small arms fire by Russian saboteurs. Cameraman Richie Mockler took two rounds to his body armor. If it weren't for his protective vest, he'd probably be dead.

Reporter Stuart Ramsay was hit in the lower back, but survived. He later said, "We were in shock, no doubt about it. But elated to be alive. Martin [Vowles, producer,] said to me, "'It's a miracle any of us got out, let alone all five of us.'"[1]

Since the outbreak of the invasion in late February, the sale of body armor and ballistic helmets has skyrocketed around the world. And demand outstrips supply. While a tranche of nations has sent tens of thousands of sets of protective vests and military-grade helmets to Ukraine, the demand on the battlefield remains high.

Law enforcement agencies and military groups across America are also donating their gear to the Ukrainian cause. These agencies are able to donate the vests as the equipment cycles through the end of manufacturers' warranties.[2] The vests are still useful, however, and any protection is vastly better than none.

That is what happened in the case of one former U.S. soldier who felt led to donate his protective vest. After he removed his ID tags and other identifying marks, he donated the vest to Gale, Johnny and Ira's colleague from Kyiv. Like the Semeniuks, Gale had evacuated to Poland once the February invasion started. On a recent trip to visit family in Chicago, Gale took possession of the vest, along with eleven boxes of humanitarian aid, and brought it all back with him to Poland.

About the same time, word came from a mutual friend in Ukraine whose brother was headed back to his town of Irpin to fight the invading Russians. He was in dire need of protective gear—the battle there involved close-range fighting, sometimes street to street with small arms fire. So the question wasn't about the need, but about the means by which Gale could get the vest to the soldier in Irpin. At that time in mid-March, the Russians were making a heavy push toward Kyiv but had stalled out in the outlying towns to the west. It was suburban areas like Irpin and Bucha that saw the heaviest fighting—and the worst atrocities.

Now it was time to arrange for delivery—but how do civilians two hours from the Ukrainian border get body armor transferred across hundreds of kilometers of unsafe roads peppered by fire fights, air strikes, and artillery shells? The plan was to enlist the help of the International Police Association drivers who had been helping the Semeniuks and Gale get aid across the border and into Ukraine. One of the IPA drivers drove the vest and the aid to the border, where Ira's brother, Yuri, picked it up.

From there, a female friend was supposed to drive from Mukachevo to Lviv, which is about four hours away, to retrieve the vest. However, Yuri decided to drive halfway to meet this friend, because shelling was taking place in and around Lviv, and it wasn't safe for her to make the entire drive. After meeting Yuri halfway at a prearranged location, the friend drove the vest and the aid back to Mukachevo (one of Ukraine's westernmost cities, which has so far remained untouched by Russian bombs). There, she had a rare chance to catch a single special bus that was making its way to Kyiv—a treacherous journey of more than 750 kilometers.

That bus then drove across central Ukraine, where it averted hot spots, skirted Russian troop movements, and arrived at a forward command position outside Irpin, where the vest was left with specific instructions including the soldier's name and unit. The vest was then hand-delivered to the intended soldier—who was grateful to have the added protection of a military-grade plated vest.

At that point, says Ira, "We kept the soldier in our prayers. We prayed that God would not only use the armor to protect him, but that a spiritual shield would surround him." While there are tens of thousands of men and women fighting in defense of Ukraine, the Semeniuks felt a sense of comradery with their "armored soldier," and God kept him on their hearts.

Just two days after the delivery of the body armor, the soldier's sister received a photo from a friend who is serving in close proximity to her brother. She then forwarded the photo to Johnny and Gale. When they opened it, they were shocked. It was a photo of the front plate of body armor, which the soldier had removed from the inner sleeve of the vest. The plate was riddled with one-inch divots and shrapnel markings. The olive vest was resting against a chair next to the armor, with a fair amount of blood visible in the top left corner—above the soldier's heart.

The photo spoke a thousand words. Of a soldier whose life was saved by the newly donned protective vest. Of an injury of unknown severity to his upper body. The Semeniuks later received word that the injury was not life-threatening.

The twisted and marred armor plate also spoke of prayers answered. Of a young man who would live to fight another day. Of the power of hope—the hope and belief of a group of friends who felt that it was worth it to procure one protective vest for one soldier fighting for a purpose greater than the sum total of all their efforts.

CHAPTER 11

Gennadiy Mokhnenko

Gennadiy Mokhnenko has a soldier's bearing. Broad-shouldered and barrel-chested with intense eyes and a rugged face, he cuts an impressive figure in his army fatigues and boots. Like many soldiers who have fought long and hard, he carries himself with quiet strength, and the battles he has fought are written in his eyes.

Gennadiy's wars, however, have not been waged with guns or bullets, and his battle scars are mostly unseen. For decades he has been waging a different kind of war in the Donetsk region against hopelessness, abandonment, and drug abuse among the region's street orphans. In 1998 he founded Republic Pilgrim to help get homeless and addicted kids off the streets of Mariupol. Since then it has grown into the largest children's rehabilitation center in Eastern Europe.

At age twenty-four Gennadiy turned to God in a time of difficulty—and God answered. He was praying for relatives bound up in alcoholism, and he saw them set free when everything else had failed. "Over time, the Lord saved both my father and mother and my sister," he said.[1] He was able to see his parents embrace God before they died, and his sister continues to do well.

In the early 1990s Gennadiy left a promising job in the book business to become a pastor. In 1992 he and some friends founded the Church of Good Changes in Mariupol, where he still serves as senior pastor. He says, "I was a homeless Christian and a homeless pastor in the first years. Maybe this is the reason why my life is connected with street kids."[2] Since then, the Protestant pastor and his church have aligned with the Church of God in Ukraine.

Mariupol is a city of more than five hundred thousand people, and Gennadiy saw a huge need in scores of children with varying problems: orphans with no parents or family; children from broken or dysfunctional homes, with little or no supervision; runaways; and kids addicted to drugs and alcohol. "At first in the 'Republic Pilgrim' there were 90% of children with punctured veins, necks, some even injected [with drugs] in the groin. There were a lot of children with AIDS, and we buried many," he says.[3]

Gennadiy is Russian-Ukrainian and his ancestry crosses national boundaries. His mother was from near St. Petersburg, and his father was from the Kursk region, an oblast of Russia that borders Ukraine. Like many other Russians and Ukrainians, the branches of his family tree stretch across the borders of both countries, and his roots run deep into Russia's cultural soil. "I grew up on Dostoevsky, Chekhov, Bulgakov, and Solzhenitsyn. I did my army service in the Moscow garrison of the fire department," he says.[4]

Like his family's history, his heart for orphans reaches beyond borders. In 2011 he helped lead a campaign called World Without Orphans—partnering with the organization of the same name—to raise global awareness for orphans. Gennadiy and several of his sons rode bikes from Ukraine all the way across far-east Russia. That trip covered more than fifteen thousand kilometers and was done in phases over four summers. Along the way, Gennadiy and his team spoke to tens of thousands of people at prearranged gatherings, while several hundred thousand more heard the message of adoption through local and regional media campaigns. Wherever they went, they received reports of people who made the decision to foster and adopt children in response to their message.[5]

The World Without Orphans campaign, with assistance from longtime Republic Pilgrim supporter Serving Orphans Worldwide, continued in 2017 when Gennadiy and his team rode across Europe, and again in 2018 when the cycling team traversed the United States.

"I dream of a world without orphans," Gennadiy says. And he has been doing his personal part to realize that dream for more than twenty years. He and his wife, Lena, have thirty-eight children, including three biological kids and thirty-five whom they've adopted. But they see no difference between those from within their family tree and those who have been grafted in by God.

Ukraine is home to approximately one hundred thousand children living in orphanages and institutions.[6] Not all of these children are orphans according to the traditional definition (i.e., a child whose parents are dead). In the last several decades the term "social orphans" has come to represent a swath of children whose parents are still alive, but who for myriad reasons are unable or unwilling to care for their children. Extreme poverty, addiction, and abandonment are all culprits. This phenomenon is not uncommon in Ukraine, and these children are said to be the victims of Fallen Leaf syndrome—blown by the winds of broken families or societal difficulties.

Since the Republic Pilgrim safehouse began nearly twenty-five years ago, more than four thousand street kids and "fallen leaves" have received help through the nonprofit organization. It is also one of the leaders of the Ukrainian movement called

"You Will Be Found," which works to educate the country about foster options and traditional adoption opportunities.

The natural outgrowth of helping these marginalized and orphaned children is to give them healthy homes that reflect the unconditional love of Christ, and thus several foster homes have been established. One home is specifically aimed at helping HIV-positive kids—the only center of its kind in the former Soviet Union.

Republic Pilgrim is more than a rehab house. It includes everything to help homeless children feel at home. Tidy, bright rooms house five to six kids each, and the multifunctional center includes a dining room, an assembly hall and rec room, computer stations, a medical office, school classrooms, a playground, and a soccer field.

Republic Pilgrim was picking up boys as young as eight and nine who were already hooked on alcohol and drugs. To get to one of the roots of the problem, Gennadiy and his team took on the illicit drug trade in the Donetsk region, working closely with police and other authorities. Their efforts worked. According to local journalists, drug dealers were losing about two million dollars a month due to this anti-drug campaign. Though Gennadiy and his team are under constant threat of reprisal, the work carries on under God's protection.[7]

In addition to helping children, Gennadiy founded a whole network of rehabilitation centers for adults. The most recent is a home called Young Mother that helps single moms who find themselves in tough circumstances.

In 2014, shortly after Russia annexed nearby Crimea, Gennadiy sat in his office and said, "If Putin entered Crimea, then why not our region? It's the same logic. They're going to bring their troops here. Europe won't make a difference, and no one will get involved."[8] Shortly thereafter, the Russians backed the separatists in Donetsk and Luhansk, and the civil war crept ever closer to the city limits of Mariupol.

While many might see events in Ukraine over the past eight years as disconnected—including the Crimean annexation, the War in Donbas, and Russia's February 2022 invasion—Gennadiy is quick to disabuse outsiders of that notion. He notes that Putin has long had his eye on the prize that is Mariupol. As the land gateway between Russia and Crimea, it seemed only a matter of time before the city was targeted (see "At the Gates of Mariupol," chapter 4).

On Victory Day, May 9, 2014—the sixty-ninth anniversary of the Soviet Union's victory over the Nazis—Mariupol was burning and people were being killed in the city center. This time, it was Russia that had brought war to Gennadiy's city. "I was ready to take up arms and go to protect my children. But thank God, I did not have to remove my pastoral rank and become a soldier, because the defenders of Ukraine successfully coped with this task without me. I am a chaplain of the Ukrainian army and now I fulfill my spiritual duties to serve Ukrainian soldiers and people in the front lines," he said.[9]

As the War in Donbas ground on, Gennadiy and his family could peer out their window and see the trenches just seven hundred meters away, and the front line was just beyond. When the rocket launchers work, you can hear everything. His children ages eight and under have known nothing but war their entire lives. "All their childhood is war," he said.

Four of his adopted sons are soldiers, including one who at twenty-five has already buried five of his friends. One of his son's friends, a nineteen-year-old boy, was killed by a Russian soldier. "My son tried to resuscitate him, until he realized that he was wiping brain off his face. This guy was an only child in the family," the pastor says.

On February 14, 2022, with two hundred thousand Russian forces massed along the borders of Russia and Belarus, Gennadiy made a fervent plea to Russian fathers and mothers via video address. As a native Russian speaker and someone who has worked in Russia on behalf of orphans, he felt compelled to speak out. Staring hard into the camera, he said,

> Dear fathers and mothers of Russian soldiers, the situation is such that in a large-scale war your sons will be thrown *en masse* into the hellfire that the Kremlin has started. And then, even as a [pastor] I will have no choice but to take up arms and stand up for my children. So please do everything you can before it's too late. Stand up to this madness! . . . Don't send your kids to the meat grinder! . . . In these anxious days, and like many of my fellow Ukrainians, I will sign up for the Territorial Defense. If the Kremlin does not stop, we will defend our land and freedom! The price may be very high, but freedom is never given in vain.[10]

Ten days after Gennadiy recorded the video, his fears were realized when Russian forces launched a full-scale invasion on several fronts across Ukraine, including a fresh offensive in the Donbas region. Though the invaders were successfully expelled from areas around Kyiv, cities in the east, such as Kharkiv, and in the south, such as Mariupol and Kherson, came under constant and withering attack by air, land, and sea.

Republic Pilgrim workers quickly realized that the children under their care were not safe, so in the middle of the night of February 24 more than three hundred kids, caretakers, and staff made a dash for safety. Gennadiy says, "It was extremely quick because it was like a competition with Russian tanks that were coming from the south and trying to block the way. And I'm so happy because we won that competition with those tanks."[11]

Within a couple of days all the children had been evacuated to a safe location in northern Germany. After their marathon trek to bring the children out, Gennadiy and his team made the eighteen-hour drive back toward Mariupol to evacuate as many people as possible. They have been able to evacuate more than thirteen hundred residents from the city. Both his personal home and the Republic Pilgrim building have been occupied by Russian troops. The church, which served as a bomb shelter for a cumulative total of a thousand people, has been shelled. Though still standing, the church lies empty until that day when the city is liberated, Gennadiy notes.

March 13 brought devastating news: In Mariupol a tank shell hit the home of Gennadiy's twenty-seven-year-old adopted daughter, Vika, who was killed. She had recently moved into her first apartment—the culmination of her journey from orphan to independent adulthood.

In an April 7 interview with CNN's Anderson Cooper, Gennadiy talked about his late daughter: "She was an amazing mom to her three-year-old son. We adopted her when she was ten and I was able to take her on trips to California and Oregon." A year ago the Ukrainian government helped Vika secure her own apartment. "She was so happy," Gennadiy said. "We helped her buy furniture and she made the place her own."[12]

The indefatigable champion of Donetsk's street children describes the medieval-like siege taking place in his city as "a Russian hell." He laments, "We don't know how many people are dead—ten thousand, twenty thousand, maybe forty thousand?"[13]

On May 17 I received a report from Gennadiy's colleague, Igor Shepyeta, saying that Gennadiy and his team continue to evacuate people from some of the hottest areas in the Donetsk region. "He was with two other war chaplains in a pickup truck and they came across some women walking along the road," Igor related. "Gennadiy made his friend Albert and the other chaplain get out of the truck so he could take the women to safety in a nearby village. 'You guys hide until I get back,' he told Albert as he sped away. In the end everyone was fine."

The war is a physical and mental siege, and Gennadiy and Lena sometimes go days with no news from their four sons who are fighting in the fields and fortifications of the Donbas.

Not long after his daughter Vika was killed, Gennadiy stood in a warehouse filled with humanitarian aid, conducting an interview with Serving Orphans Worldwide. It was on what would have been Vika's twenty-eighth birthday. The organization's field coordinator, Coleman Bailey, asked him about the stakes of the war. Without pause Gennadiy said, "Ukraine will win this war because it is about our freedom. It's not about gas or land or money. We are a free nation and we will never be enslaved by Russia's KGB leaders."

With the eyes of the world fixed on Ukraine, her sons and daughters press forward. And with fighters such as Gennadiy Mokhnenko, it's not difficult to imagine that victory is not far off.

CHAPTER 12

Jhenya

Our third daughter, Zoë, was born in 2003. Her name means "life" in Greek. I was content—three girls were all I needed. But God had other plans. Around Christmas 2004 Suzanne was putting Zoë down for the night and kept hearing a baby crying. She looked outside the window but couldn't figure out where the cries were coming from. Suzanne felt prompted to pray for the crying child. The next night as she put Zoë to bed, she heard the crying baby again. She questioned God and asked, *God, I've been praying for neglected children, but why do I keep hearing crying?*

God simply replied, *I want you to adopt.*

The third night, when she was putting Zoë to bed, she questioned God and asked, *Whom do You want us to adopt?*

God spoke to her in His still, small voice, and the words were very specific: *I want you to adopt a child from Ukraine. It is to be a boy and not a baby.*

Suzanne was stunned. She thought, *Ukraine? I know that's a former Soviet Union country, but where is it exactly?* The next day she went into the basement and found Ukraine on the kids' big blue globe. She then asked a few close friends to pray about what she had heard. She kept the entire experience to herself for nearly six months. On our sixteenth wedding anniversary—May 7, 2005—she told me the entire story over dinner. She figured that I would be in a good mood; even if I didn't like the idea, at least I wouldn't make a public scene.

While I believed what she told me, I was also terrified by the idea. I told her I was scared to bring an older male child into our home. Wouldn't it be better to adopt a baby boy? Suzanne was polite but firm: "No, God was very clear, and this is what He told me." My wife is not the type of person who walks into a room and says, "God spoke to me and said . . ." I knew she was sincere.

Several months went by, and we didn't talk much about the adoption idea. One evening in the summer, Suzanne casually said, "I meant to tell you that an international adoption agency called America World is hosting an information meeting at church this Tuesday. Do you want to go?"

"Sure," I said, without much thought.

The America World presenter showed a brief video clip by Steven Curtis Chapman, the Nashville-based music artist who has adopted several children. In fact, he and his wife, Mary Beth, have six children—three biological children and three adopted daughters from China. As Chapman sat on his front porch and talked about his adoption journey, he emphasized that he had read the passage in James 1 a hundred times where it says to take care of orphans and widows. But then one day he read it and knew it was an assignment. God was calling him to adopt, and he had a choice either to obey the call or ignore it.

In that moment, as the artist shared those words, I remember thinking, *Duncan, you have two choices: accept God's assignment or disobey Him.* On the drive home I shared my experience with Suzanne, and soon after, we kicked things into high gear regarding the adoption. Interestingly enough, what we did not know beforehand is that America World was one of the only U.S.-based adoption agencies that worked in Ukraine. By summer 2007, after two years of paperwork, FBI background checks, home visits from various social workers, and many starts and stops, we were ready to leave for Ukraine.

Two weeks before our scheduled departure for Kyiv we received bad news: A biopsy confirmed that Suzanne had breast cancer. An MRI further revealed that the cancer had spread to at least two lymph nodes. And the more doctors we spoke with, the more confused we became. One told us that this was one of the worst types of breast cancer and that we should cancel our adoption plans. Another asked Suzanne, "How many children do you have, and how old are they?" intimating that it was time for Suzanne to get her affairs in order.

Finally, we met with the lead oncologist, Dr. Eric Weinshel, who heard our entire story, our adoption plans, and our anguish over not knowing what to do. He was blunt but kind: "This tumor, while serious, is slow growing," he said in his New York accent. "Go to Ukraine, get your son, and come back in a couple of weeks to start chemotherapy."

I asked, "By doing this adoption and waiting, will it hurt Suzanne's chances of recovery?"

Dr. Weinshel didn't hesitate: "No, two weeks won't put her at greater risk, and she is fine to go. But I have a question for you," he pressed, looking at me intently. "Even though she has an 85 percent chance of recovery, are you ready to be a widower and a single dad to four kids, in case the worst happens?"

I lied and said I was.

On July 15 my wife, three daughters, nineteen-year-old niece, and I boarded a KLM flight for Kyiv via Munich. Suzanne and I were carrying $18,000 cash in the form of 180 crisp, new $100 bills split between us. International adoption is not cheap. And in Ukraine, you wait a week for a document, or you pay a Benjamin and get it within an hour. (In the United States we call such transactions a service fee—the cultural equivalent in Ukraine.) Upon our arrival at Boryspil International Airport we met Yuri Safonov, our adoption facilitator. Yuri would turn out to be a godsend—a negotiator, fixer, and ingenious eliminator of red tape.

Our flat half a block off Maidan Square was old, elegant, and high ceilinged. From this central location we got to know the city center. It felt far from a vacation, and it was hard to relax with the cancer diagnosis hanging over our heads. As well, we didn't want to tell our girls until our return to Minneapolis, so that was an added layer of stress.

The timing of our trip was based on our appointment with the State Department of Adoption, which had been set months prior for 4:00 p.m. Wednesday, July 18. We were hoping to see at least three viable profiles, and actually were able to look at eight. We were told we had thirty minutes to make a decision. I had the strangest thought: *Thirty minutes? We aren't picking carpet swatches here.*

One boy was too young, another was too old, and a few had some health concerns. The profiles consisted of a duplexed piece of paper tucked into a thin plastic sleeve, with vitals, medical information, and a brief description written in Cyrillic. So there we were, sitting in this little upstairs office in the old part of Kyiv, in a hot, stuffy room with three Ukrainian officials looking at us while we tried to decide between two little boys' profiles.

I asked if Yuri could join us from the adjoining room to translate the documents. One official gave me a puzzled look and left. A moment later Yuri entered, looking a little surprised as the officials left the room. We had about twenty minutes left to make a choice, so Yuri quickly translated the details and medical reports for each boy. Sweat slid down my neck as Suzanne and I stared at the profiles, somewhat immobilized by the stifling heat and enormity of the decision. I stared hard at the Ukrainian text, as if by doing so an invisible key might slide into place and unlock the answer.

Suzanne knew right away when she saw one boy's picture that he was the one we were supposed to adopt. I liked another boy who, like me, suffered from asthma. The officials reentered the room and looked at us, as if to say, "Well, what's it going to be?" After about ten minutes more of this, we asked if we could be alone to make a decision. The trio seemed relieved to retreat to the other office, where they sipped lukewarm Cokes and stood in front of a large metal fan, small silver slips of aluminum foil fluttering in the artificial breeze.

With Yuri's translation skills and a bit more discussion, Suzanne and I agreed that a little boy named Jhenya looked very good. The other little guy had two siblings still living with the mother, and we didn't want to split up a family that might have a chance to reunite one day, whereas Jhenya had no siblings with his mother. Jhenya's mischievous grin, brown eyes, and dirty blond hair looked up at us from his photo as we announced our decision to meet Jhenya to see if it was a fit. The officials smiled and handed us warm Cokes.

When we left the building Yuri told us that in the dozens of adoptions he had facilitated, he had never been allowed in the room while the parents made their decision. It was the first of many *malen'ki dyva*—small miracles—in our adoption journey.

Within twenty-four hours we had arranged for travel from Kyiv to Mariupol, the location of Jhenya's orphanage. For this next phase of the process, we were introduced to Igor Eros, who would serve as our highly capable facilitator on our trip south, while Yuri coordinated things from Kyiv. Two days after making our decision we flew into Donetsk International Airport, which is about two hours north of Mariupol. This is the same airport that became a symbolic slice of highly contested real estate that changed hands several times in 2014 at the start of the Donbas civil war, and was eventually bombed into ruins.

At the time, Mariupol was a thriving port city on the Sea of Azov, and one of Ukraine's most vital shipping centers. After a day, we found an apartment big enough to accommodate our family of five, plus Igor and our niece Emily. She had come with us to serve as an au pair while Suzanne and I were running around town chasing down this document and that. The apartment building was in the ubiquitous Brezhnev-era concrete block style of the 1970s that you see throughout Ukraine and other former Soviet republics. It is most likely destroyed now.

The next day, we head out to visit Jhenya for the first time at the orphanage. The drive there takes you east out of the city center, along Naberezhna Street, the Kalmius River on your left, and the massive Azovstal iron and steel works on your right. It's a sweltering summer day, and children and their parents are cooling themselves in the river. The Sonechko ("Ladybug") Children's Home is a few kilometers farther along, tucked inside a quiet, leafy neighborhood on the eastern outskirts of Mariupol. Its grounds are tidy, its buildings freshly painted and smart. Sandboxes and jungle gyms dot the shaded property. Igor says it's one of the nicest orphanages he has ever visited. When we pull up to the front of the building about twenty little ones in bathing suits are taking turns swimming in a small plastic pool.

The orphanage director is a smartly dressed, dignified woman in her early forties who describes Jhenya as a healthy, smart little boy—a standout in the orphanage. She says his mother was not an addict of any kind, but rather, was often out of the country with work. During those times she would drop off Jhenya with friends or relatives and leave him for long stretches of time. He was born in Bilytske, a village northwest of Donetsk.

The relatives and friends had growing concerns for Jhenya's welfare, and after the mother failed to appear in court her parental rights were terminated. Contrary to what we'd been told, we learned that Cory actually does have a younger brother named Oleg. In 2006 the brothers were separated and moved to different orphanages. Today our son has no recollection of his younger brother, who was adopted by a Canadian family only a few months prior to when we met Jhenya in August 2007. So there is the possibility of a future reunion.

After the meeting with the director, we went out into the play yard and were able to see Jhenya from a distance, just interacting with the other kids naturally, not knowing we were there. He hugged the female worker/teacher several times while we were watching. Then we approached him, and he came up to us as Igor explained that we wanted to meet him. He immediately gave us big hugs and said, "I want a mama and papa, and if you do not take me, I will run away and find my own mama, papa, and *babusya* [grandma]."

We spent about an hour with Jhenya, chatting and playing, and left him with two small toys that he liked very much. The experience was positive, though overwhelming. Here you are with this little guy, and in your head you are saying, *Is this our son?*

We left that afternoon with the orphanage director, the city's social worker, and Igor asking us what we planned to do. We told them that we needed some time and that we'd give them a decision the following day.

In retrospect, as I think about this seminal moment in our family's life, I'm reminded of a blog post I had written just before leaving for Ukraine. I had just finished reading *The Painted Veil* by Somerset Maugham, in which English bacteriologist Walter Fane and his wife, Kitty, move to a remote region of China to combat a cholera outbreak. The wife is drifting on the heels of an affair, unsure of her love for Walter. Toward the end of the novel, and in response to Kitty's claim that sticking with her husband has to do with duty, the mother superior of the local French convent says,

> Remember that it is nothing to do your duty, that is demanded of you and is no more meritorious than to wash your hands when they are dirty; the only thing that counts is the love of duty; when love and duty are one, then grace is in you and you will enjoy a happiness which passes all understanding.[1]

We had been led to adopt a boy, and we were doing our best to obey that assignment. There is no virtue signaling in that statement. In fact, to be candid, the opposite is true: Neither Suzanne nor I was driven by emotion or sentiment. We had already lost three children to miscarriage and a newborn son to a rare genetic disorder called trisomy 13. We had been in the valley, had walked its dark corners, and had suffered—as had our older girls, Hannah and Kylie. We were content with our three girls; we didn't pine for another child. Yet God spoke unequivocally.

I could pick up the story at the orphanage and describe how we finally agreed that Jhenya was the boy that God meant for our family. I could describe how Suzanne flew home with the girls after two weeks—the shortest legalized adoption Yuri had ever facilitated—and I stayed in Ukraine another two weeks to finish up the paperwork and a ten-day waiting period. I could tell you how, upon Suzanne's return, she started chemotherapy, and each night before I went to sleep in the Mariupol apartment, I'd call to check in. And how I listened to her voice grow progressively weaker over those weeks. And how at times I'd cry myself to sleep, not knowing if my wife was going to survive.

No, I'll stick to the heart of the matter: We were two ordinary people who had cashed in half our 401(k) because we felt strongly that it was what God was telling us to do. It was our duty. And like Kitty Fane, we were struggling with that duty. How do you love a stranger? And is there something wrong if an adoptive parent does not have an instantaneous connection with and love for an orphaned child?

As adoptive parents we've met others who did have an instantaneous and highly emotional connection with their adoptive child. Most, in fact. But we did not. It took time. But eventually, what started out as just duty turned into the love of duty. And the grace found there is bountiful. The journey we've been on, however, has not been easy. I'm very grateful to say that Suzanne beat her cancer and is now fifteen years cancer-free.

Cory Jhenya Duncan is now twenty-one years old. The thin, wiry kid with boundless energy has grown into a strong man with a Ukrainian spirit—tough, courageous, and unsinkable. If he had the money he'd be on a plane to Poland tomorrow and then on a train to Lviv to join Ukraine's fight. In fact, we've been told he would be conscripted into the army because he's native born. He struggles with the what-ifs of a birth mom he hopes to meet one day. Cory hopes for a reunion with his brother, Oleg, as well.

Rather than Cory joining the Ukrainian Army, however, I think I've talked him into waiting until this horrible war ends, so we can go there together. By that time Cory will have finished a two-year welding certification program, and his metal-working skills will be greatly needed in Ukraine's reconstruction.

When we are there I want to drive to Bilytske, and we will try to reconnect with his birth mom. In the meantime, we do what we can through prayers and donations for the people of Mariupol. We talk about the outnumbered and surrounded soldiers who held out for three months beneath the Azovstal iron and steel works. I show Cory pictures of the massive steel works that I took when we were there in 2007. What we don't talk about much are the horrors taking place in Mariupol—it's just too hard for Cory to hear. An estimated twenty thousand civilians dead, mass graves identified on the city's outskirts.

My son is the most giving person I've ever met. I burst with pride thinking about him. His life, however, has been very difficult. He was dealt a tough hand, and we are doing everything we can to help position him for his best chance of success. His future is uncertain—as are yours and mine. And certainly for the people of Donetsk Oblast, the region where Cory comes from, where some of the war's heaviest fighting is happening right now.

As I mentioned, the Azovstal iron and steel works was on the route to Cory's orphanage, and I passed it at least a dozen times. During the first three months of the war, when I saw the news of soldiers and civilians holding out in the bunkers beneath the massive smokestacks and factory buildings, it brought me back to Mariupol. Is Sonechko orphanage still there? I found the phone number on Google and tried to call; there was no answer. Where is the orphanage director, or Cory's favorite caretaker, Ilya, who cried when she said good-bye to Cory? Where is Vanya, Cory's best friend there? Is he fighting on the front lines? Are some of the other boys and girls, who would now be around twenty, fighting, too?

Like the lines from Maugham's powerful novel, I do believe that when love and duty are one, then grace is in us and we will enjoy "a happiness which passes all understanding." I can relate to that line now, much more so than when I wrote my blog post fifteen years ago. Amid the heartache and pain—both because of it, and in spite of it—I also know that God is there for Cory. I know that as certainly as I know the sun will rise tomorrow.

I once heard musician and iconoclast Charlie Peacock say that we can only possess what we experience. I agree. Experience, however, exposes our weaknesses and lays bare our faults. As C. S. Lewis said in the movie *Shadowlands*, "Experience is a most brutal teacher. But you learn, my God you learn."[2]

Experience is also a banner—unique to each of us—into which God stitches intimate words of love and hope and grace. And as each of our banners fly, the depth and breadth of His love are displayed.

Cory's banner is made of strong fabric—it is battle-tested, frayed, but tough. I believe it is yet to be fully unfurled, and as his dad, I look forward to watching it fly.

CHAPTER 13

Colonel Korenevych

Like an apple sliced by a sharp knife, the two halves of life for Colonel Valentyn Korenevych are clearly defined.

The first half of his life began in Kazakhstan, where he pursued a career in the Army of the Soviet Socialist Republics. It was 1983, the height of the Cold War and the year Ronald Reagan referred to the USSR as the evil empire. A year earlier the American president had boldly predicted that the Soviet Union would be consigned to the ash heap of history.[1]

For Comrade Korenevych, those were fighting words. He was a committed communist with a promising future in the Soviet Army's logistics branch. After four years of military school he was assigned to a post in Taldykorgan, not far from Kazakhstan's border with China. He and his wife, Marina, soon started a family and were content to raise their children in the Soviet manner.

And then came the collapse of the USSR, and major decisions had to be made. He asked his wife, "What direction would you like to take? Where do you want to live?"

It was 1992 and a time of major upheaval as the former Soviet military structure was reinventing itself now as the Russian military. He was a communist who had been trained in the Soviet military mindset. Now he had to decide if he would stay in the Russian army or go elsewhere.

The colonel describes the difficulty he faced: "The Soviet military had made every decision for me. I did not have to think. They told me what to do and where to go." After much consideration, he and Marina decided to go to Chernihiv, Ukraine, where his parents lived.

Little did the colonel know that their decision would radically alter the course of their lives. Thus began the second half of life for Colonel Korenevych.

He retired from the Soviet Army and came to Ukraine, where he decided to make a second oath—this time to the Ukrainian people and as an officer in the Ukrainian Army. "It was not an easy decision because the spirit of communism was very strong," he says. Many of his fellow officers refused to join; they had made an oath under the Soviet hammer and sickle, and could not make a second oath to the Ukrainian shield and trident.

While the colonel's decision to serve in the Ukrainian army was significant, it was not the decision that best divides the first half of his life from the second. The prologue to that decision came in 1991 in that frontier town on the edge of Kazakhstan, when a Baptist church gave him a copy of the New Testament.

At that world-altering moment of the twentieth century, as the edifice of Soviet communism was imploding, Colonel Korenevych's destiny shifted. God nudged him off the familiar path he had been following as a Soviet Army officer and recalibrated his navigational course. The nudge was in the form of a Kazakh New Testament, and over the course of the next few years, the magnetic pull of that Book's words caused the colonel's sense of true north to move.

When Colonel Korenevych made the 3,500-kilometer journey from central Asia to Eastern Europe, he left behind more than his green-and-red Soviet uniform. He and his family were leaving a culture and ideology that they had previously never questioned. And though the change came slowly, it did come.

Soon the family became Ukrainian citizens and settled into their new life as the colonel served in a military brigade near Kyiv. Five years later, Korenevych was assigned to Kyiv's military school of communications while he completed his studies at Taras Shevchenko University.

After the fall of the Soviet Union, all types of religious groups flowed into the vacuum left behind by seventy-five years of atheist ideology. Among the groups were the Jehovah's Witnesses, who reached out to the colonel and his wife around 1997. "They gave us their journals, and we wanted to see God in those materials. But we didn't know which God," the colonel says.

Eventually things came to a head between the couple. They were looking for God, but were confused about which group or doctrine was best for them. Was it the Jehovah's Witnesses, the Orthodox belief, or another way? "One night we were really conflicted about this problem, so we prayed that the first person who came to our house and invited us to church was how we would decide. No questions asked. We would just go."

The following day a military wife who lived nearby came to their home and invited them to church. They didn't know the name of the church or anything about it, but they went. "When the church found out that we had been considering the Jehovah's Witnesses, they were concerned. They told us that we needed to repent and ask Jesus into our lives," the colonel says. "We visited this church for a year, and they always talked about the importance of repentance. So after a year, we repented." In 2000 he and Marina and three hundred other people from the church were baptized in the Dnipro River.

Up to this point Colonel Korenevych did not believe people in the military could be Christians. He had never known any other Christian officers, and of course, the Soviet Army hadn't officially allowed it. "Now we were meeting all types of Christians in the Ukrainian military, and it was an eye-opener," he says.

Around this time the colonel met American Bruce Kittleson, co-founder of Olive Branch International (OBI), a nongovernmental organization (NGO) founded shortly after the fall of the Soviet Union. OBI provides humanitarian services to the international military community and works in more than fifteen nations across several continents with rabbis, priests, monks, imams, and pastors from every denominational background.

Shortly after the two men met, adds the colonel, "Bruce asked me a strange question. He said, 'Do you want to start a military chaplain program at Kyiv Theological Seminary?' I told him that I was an officer of logistics, not a military chaplain. And I had never heard this phrase before and knew nothing about the work. And he said, 'That's easy. I'll just take you to the United States for three weeks to learn.'"

During the first half of the colonel's life, a trip to the United States would have only occurred under a flag of war. "The only thing I wanted to do as a Soviet officer was hurt my American enemy," he says. "We were indoctrinated to hate everything about America, and here I was about to go there."

During their three weeks in America in 2007 Bruce took the colonel to several installations, including a naval base and a military hospital. The colonel soaked up as much as he could, and the trip made a significant impression on him. Even more than the information he received, he found the inspiration and vision to build a military chaplaincy program back in Ukraine.

"It was a great trip, but everywhere I went people gave me English books. However, I did not read English. When I got to the airport my bags were too heavy, so I chose to keep several jars of peanut butter and leave the books behind," he quips.

It was hard to find peanut butter in Ukraine; books you could always get your hands on.

The colonel explains the importance of that trip: "I've had three major changes in my mind during my life. The first was when I gave up the communist mindset and made my vow to the Ukrainian army. The second was when I gave my life to God. And the third was when I went to America."

The next chapter in the colonel's life involved his decision to attend Irpin Biblical Seminary to earn a divinity degree. "I was still fascinated with the question, Can a military person be a Christian? So my master's degree work was centered on this idea of believers in the armed services. And that is how the chaplain program started at Kyiv Theological Seminary."

The colonel now works as a professor at the seminary, where he also earned his master's degree in theology. He is also president of Olive Branch Ukraine and senior pastor of Way of Truth Church in Kyiv.

Olive Branch Ukraine works closely with the Ukrainian military fellowship, and with the chaplaincies of Ukrainian Protestant and historical churches. There are many needs, and over the last twenty years God has used all these groups to build a network of spiritual support for Ukraine's military.

As someone who spent a decade serving as a logistics officer in the Soviet Army, Colonel Korenevych understands the structure and mindset of Russia's invasion in Ukraine. "The Soviet Army and the Russian Army are the same. It is the same spirit today that drove communism thirty years ago," he says. "There are thousands of officers in the Russian Army today who are just the way I used to be. It is not a godly structure."

Since the war broke out the colonel has been juggling many priorities: teaching his seminary courses online; providing for the ever-changing needs of his church in a time of war; working with the war chaplains who are serving on the front lines; and staying in close contact with the four sons he and Marina raised. "When I go on Facebook, one out of every three posts is about someone who has died," he says.

His mother's apartment in Chernihiv was struck by three missiles, and forty-nine people were killed by just one of the strikes. "The only reason my mother is alive is that she was in her bathroom when the nearest missile struck." Like millions of others across Ukraine, his mother has lost her home and many of her friends.

One of the biggest challenges the colonel and other military chaplains face is helping soldiers struggling with thoughts of revenge. It's difficult to look a soldier in the eye who has just lost his best friend to a Russian tank shell, he notes. "That is our job, though, so we pray for God's guidance and the leading of the Holy Spirit in these tough times."

Colonel Korenevych is quick to point out that God is active in the trenches of the Donbas. "Today we had an online gathering of about eighty-five chaplains, and we discussed this question about how God is at work even amid the horrible death and destruction. So this is not my opinion, but the stories that are coming in from chaplains all across the front lines. The soldiers say that when a chaplain is nearby, it's a guarantee that a missile will not fall on them." The consensus is that the vast majority of soldiers are very open to God and readily ask chaplains to pray with them.

"Many will ask a chaplain just to sit with them during their night watch," the colonel adds. "Everywhere we go along the front lines of Ukraine the men and women soldiers say that there is this unique, unifying spirit that they can't explain. We can then say that what they are sensing are the prayers of believers in Ukraine and around the world. This is a great encouragement and support to them." Senior officers even request that chaplains be posted in their field of command. "When a chaplain is with their troops, they report less drinking, profanity, and bad behavior," he says.

The colonel observes that before Russia's February invasion, you didn't really hear President Volodymyr Zelensky talk about God. Zelensky was a comedian and television actor before he ran for president. And in a surreal example of life imitating art, the show he starred in just prior to running for office was based on a schoolteacher's unlikely rise to the position of Ukrainian president. "Before the invasion I only saw our president in comic situations where he joked about God," the colonel says. "But during the war he started talking about God, and he attended church."

Colonel Korenevych sees a stark difference between the unified spirit present throughout Ukraine and what is happening in Russia. With his history of having served in both the Soviet and Ukrainian armies, he has the knowledge and experience to understand the mindset of both sides of this present conflict.

"I think God wants to achieve several goals through this war. The first is to motivate His people to pray and to prepare for the Second Coming of Christ. We live in a time when the Antichrist will come from one side, and God is preparing us for this. But from the other side, God prepares something opposite. God's other goal in this war is to destroy the antichrist spirit in Moscow and even in Ukraine, where many people still have a Soviet world mentality," he says.

The two halves of life for Colonel Korenevych have revealed that, at his core, he desires to see people grow closer to God. "In our organization," he says, "we say that God changes hearts through the olive branch. That is my prayer during these difficult days of war, and for whatever comes after."

CHAPTER 14

Tatiana, Bogdan, and Masha

Each day at 3:00 p.m. Tatiana Sakovska greets her students for the theater class she teaches online with a large smile. Her pupils—ranging in age from eight to eighteen—are from all across Europe. One young boy joins from a basement in Mykolaiv. Sometimes during the class the other members can hear the sounds of bombs in the background. His mother tells Tatiana that her class is the one sane, normal thing in her son's life, and he looks forward to it every day.

Other children are from cities most of us have heard of on the news—including Mykolaiv, Odesa, and the city of Kherson, which is now under Russian occupation. Some of Tatiana's students have fled Ukraine for Poland and elsewhere throughout Europe—a diaspora of budding actors, all affected by the war in one way or another. But every day at 3:00 p.m., seven days a week, for one hour life is about art and the imagination, and the war goes away for just a little while.

"I used to do the class four days a week," says Tatiana. "But now we do it every day because it's so important for the children to get a break from the war. Our time is all about joyful things, about creativity. No one is allowed to use the W word," she says with a smile.

Tatiana is an actress herself, and before the war she enjoyed a full life in the beautiful seaside town of Odesa, along with her husband, Bogdan, and her teen daughter, Masha. Both she and Bogdan are recognizable faces on Ukrainian television, and they met through Odesa's thriving theater community. Sixteen-year-old Masha—who is both an actress and a model—had just begun acting in a short film before the war started. She plans to resume her acting career when the war is over.

When the war came, mother and daughter decided to join Tatiana's cousin, Natasha Olshanska, who was leaving for Poland with her sixteen-year-old son, Jhenya. Natasha works as an international adoption facilitator and has helped evacuate nearly twenty orphans and several caregivers from Vinnytsia in central Ukraine. (See more about Natasha and Jhenya in chapter 3, "The Hunting Lodge.") The two cousins are like sisters, and they have been close since they were small children. "We did not know where we would go," says Tatiana, "and so when Natasha asked me to join her, I knew it was the right thing for my daughter and me—until that day when the war ends and we will reunite with Bogdan."

During World War II the cousins' common grandmother, Nadezhda, escaped the Nazis with her cousin. Eighty years later, family history repeats itself as Tatiana and Natasha flee Ukraine—but this time from Russian bombs rather than German.

As I related in chapter 3, on a snowy Sunday in early April I visit the stately manor house where Tatiana, Masha, Natasha, and Jhenya are staying, along with the orphans who range in age from two to eighteen, and also several female caretakers. It is a beautiful manor house the caregivers call "the hunting lodge" that has been offered rent-free by a local Polish hotelier. The fully renovated home sits on several acres in the countryside east of Warsaw and is accessed by a long, tree-lined lane. The sounds of the village beyond the manor's grounds are silenced by the quiet falling snow.

As we talk over black tea with sugar, Tatiana glances at her phone, smiles excitedly, and darts into an adjoining room. Natasha tells me that before Tatiana decided to leave Odesa and join her and her son in Poland, she was very worried for her cousin. "At that time, we were fearing that the Russians would try a marine assault on Odesa from the Black Sea," she says.

With the sinking of several Russian ships—including their flagship cruiser, the *Moskva*, in mid-April—fears of an amphibious invasion of Odesa have subsided somewhat. Now, between caring for nearly twenty lively children, including near-daily runs to the grocery store, Natasha says that having Tatiana with her is a blessing.

"I was praying every day for Tatiana and her family, and was so worried," says Natasha. "Because we know each other so well, it makes it even that much more comforting for Masha and her to be here with us."

Several minutes later Tatiana reenters the room in a buoyant mood. She has just ended a video call with her husband, whom she has not heard from in a couple of days. She notes that it was very hard to leave Bogdan, who stayed behind to serve in Ukraine's Territorial Defense. "Sometimes I don't hear from him for several days," says Tatiana, "due to the sensitive nature of his location. It is during those times that I try to stay busy—helping the orphans here at the manor house, directing plays, and teaching my theater course online."

On that snowy Sunday evening Stasz and I are the guests of honor at the house's weekly children's play, directed by Tatiana. After a hearty meal of borsch and hot bread, we help clear the table as the kids race about, preparing for the evening's performance. Tatiana notes that such healthy diversions help not only the children, but the adults as well.

Tonight we are treated to a raucous rendition of *Thumbelina*. Fanciful costumes have been handmade from what's available, including fairy wings made of painted plastic wrap and thin strips of colorful cloth.

In the classic 1835 tale by Hans Christian Andersen, a fairy named Thumbelina must brave a harsh winter and noisome suitors before she finds an injured swallow that she nurses back to health. Feeling trapped into marrying a mole, she sees no way out until the swallow spirits her away to a distant land.

Among the colors of a beautiful flower field Thumbelina meets a fairy prince her same size, whom she marries. She finally feels at home—safe and comfortable. In the end, Thumbelina receives her own set of wings and a new name, Maia, after the Greco-Roman goddess of springtime.

It's a fitting story to share with these refugee orphans, who have braved brutal conditions in their search for a safe, secure home. And thanks to selfless people like Tatiana and Natasha, that is exactly what they have found.

CHAPTER 15

Ukraine's Deep Jewish Roots

Before World War II, approximately 1.5 million Jews lived in Ukraine. This accounted for the largest population of Jews in the USSR, and one of the largest in Europe. That number rose to 2.45 million between 1939 and 1941 due to Stalin's occupation of several adjacent territories.

The Germans, their Axis allies, and other collaborators including certain Ukrainians and supporters from Belarus would march adult male Jews into the woods and fields and shoot them. During 1941, that dark year in Ukraine's history, the killing expanded to include women and children.

In January 1942 top Reich officials met and approved what Hitler henchman Reinhard Heydrich would call the "Final Solution to the Jewish Question."[1] Meaning, extermination. But by this time, before the ghoulish use of death camps, crematoria, and gas chambers, 1.5 million men, women, and children had already been shot and killed in Ukraine—matching its entire prewar population of Jews.

This first phase of Nazi horrors against Jews in Ukraine is sometimes called the "Holocaust by Bullets." Using the country's present-day borders, one in every four Jewish victims of the Holocaust was killed in Ukraine.[2]

Jewish roots run very deep in Ukraine, and branches of Judaism have spread widely across the globe. One such branch is Hasidism, which many historians say can be traced to the eighteenth-century charismatic leader Israel ben Eliezer—better known as Baal Shem Tov—from the Ukrainian-Polish town of Medzhybizh.[3]

As well as Ukraine's imprint upon Judaism, its culture and heritage have also spread far from Ukraine. In an incisive piece for the *Kyiv Post*, journalist Matthew Kupfer says, "There would be no modern Ukraine without Jews. And there would be no State of Israel without Ukraine." He says that "for many, Ukraine is known as a place where Jews were killed [by the Nazis and the Soviet Union]." However, Kupfer notes,

> Meanwhile, fewer recognize that many of the founding fathers of Israel came from what is today Ukraine. Many are unaware that Zionism and Ukrainian nationalism both emerged as national liberation movements for minorities in the Russian Empire.
>
> Few know that Vladimir Ze'ev Jabotinsky—the founder of revisionist Zionism and the spiritual father of Israeli Prime Minister Benjamin Netanyahu's Likud Party—was a Russian-language writer from Odesa who viewed Jews and Ukrainians as allies in the struggle for democratization in the empire.[4]

These Jewish influences in Ukraine can be traced back more than sixteen hundred years. It is believed that the first Jewish settlers arrived in the fourth century in Crimea and areas along the Black Sea coast. From there they migrated throughout the region, some even converting Turkic Khazars along their journey. Eventually many settled in Kievan Rus', where by the eleventh century they had built prosperous communities.[5] Over the next few centuries, however, Jews in Ukraine would suffer greatly under the persecution of the Cossacks and the forced resettlement—called the Pale of Settlement—under Catherine the Great, to a region straddling present-day eastern Poland and western Ukraine.

The years 1917–1920 saw wave after wave of Russian and Soviet pogroms—a Russian word that means "to wreak havoc, to demolish violently"[6]—that killed more than 100,000 Ukrainian Jews. It was these pogroms that paved the wave for the Holocaust by Bullets that would occur twenty years later.

Between September 29 and 30, 1941, one of the most infamous episodes of the Nazi occupation of Ukraine occurred in Kyiv in a ravine called Babyn Yar. Before this, about 100,000 of Kyiv's 160,000 Jews had fled or had been conscripted into the Red Army.[7] The Nazis brought 33,771 of Kyiv's remaining Jews to Babyn Yar and executed them, burying them in mass graves.[8]

On March 1, 2022, during Russia's failed attempt to conquer Kyiv, a bomb fell just next to the Babyn Yar Holocaust Memorial Center, which honors the nearby site of the 1941 massacre. In response to the attack, President Volodymyr Zelensky tweeted,

> To the world: What is the point of saying "never again" for 80 years, if the world stays silent when a bomb drops on the same site of Babyn Yar? At least 5 killed. History repeating . . .[9]

One of the goals of Putin's "special military operation" in Ukraine is to "denazify" the country. The absurdity is not lost on President Zelensky, who is Jewish and lost relatives in the Holocaust. His grandfather, Semyon Ivanovich Zelensky, fought in the Soviet Union's Red Army during World War II. In a visit to his hometown of Kryvyi Rih on May 9, 2022, to celebrate Victory Day in Ukraine, President Zelensky laid red carnations on his grandfather's grave. In tribute to his grandfather's bravery, he wrote, "Thanks for the fact that the inhuman ideology of Nazism is forever a thing of the past. Thanks to those who fought against Nazism—and won."[10]

In January 2020, Zelensky flew to Israel to commemorate the seventy-fifth anniversary of the liberation of Auschwitz. In his time with Prime Minister Benjamin Netanyahu, he told stories about a Crimean Muslim woman and a Catholic priest who each saved scores of Jewish children.[11] Then he told Netanyahu a third story about a family of four brothers:

> "Three of them, their parents and their families became victims of the Holocaust. All of them were shot by German occupiers who invaded Ukraine," he said. "The fourth brother survived. . . . Two years after the war, he had a son, and in 31 years, he had a grandson. In 40 more years, that grandson became president, and he is standing before you today, Mr. Prime Minister."[12]

Like the history of the nation itself, Ukraine's story during World War II is complex and impossible to reduce to a single chapter here. A number of Ukrainians did collaborate with the German occupiers, especially at the beginning of the war. The horror of Stalin's Holodomor of the early 1930s was still fresh in the national psyche. However, the Holocaust by Bullets and other German atrocities soon turned the vast majority of Ukrainians against the Third Reich.

While 1.5 million Ukrainian Jews were executed by the Nazis, the number would have been higher but for a cadre of non-Jews who risked their lives to help. As of January 1, 2021, Yad Vashem—the World Holocaust Remembrance Center in Jerusalem—lists 2,673 Ukrainians as Righteous Among the Nations—non-Jews who risked their lives to save Jews during the Holocaust.[13]

The vast majority of those rescuers are now deceased. In fact, the New Jersey–based Jewish Foundation for the Righteous is in contact with just fifteen remaining Righteous Persons in Ukraine. The foundation sends $3,000 annually to each rescuer in three installments. (In contrast, the average Ukrainian retired person receives a pension equivalent to $101 per month.) Though the foundation was able to send the first $1,000 checks in February 2022, they decided to fast-track the rest of the year's funds to the rescuers to meet their critical wartime needs. Fluid conditions in Ukraine, however, made the distribution of the $2,000 checks difficult. It's customary for the recipient to have a "proof of life" document notarized prior to the disbursement of funds. But chasing down a notary in a war zone isn't easy, so the decision was made to have each rescuer snap and send a photo.

As well, contact with the rescuers by email was proving unfruitful, so phone calls would need to be made.[14] That's when New York attorney Dimitri Zolotkovsky, who grew up in Kyiv and speaks Russian, jumped at the chance to help. Amazingly, he was able to reach all of the rescuers, save one who died of natural causes on March 31. All the others have received their $2,000 checks.

In his gripping May 18, 2022, story in the *Jewish Standard*, reporter Stewart Ain wrote,

> The granddaughter of Olympiada D., who will be 100 in December [2022], wrote from Odessa to say thank you for the money and to also send a photo to demonstrate proof of life. The Yad Vashem database contains a listing for an Olympiada D., who was 17 when she worked with her father to shelter and feed Jewish friends of their family, including their baby, when Jews from Odessa were being deported to concentration camps.
>
> "Please excuse the quality of the photo," Olympiada's granddaughter wrote. "After the air raid we do not turn on the big light."[15]

The grandson of Aleksandra B. from Vinnytsia took his grandmother to the relative safety of a village one hundred kilometers away, where he was able to purchase much-needed medicine for her. He said, "When she receives help from you, tears of joy appear in her eyes."

He added, "I am also taking care of the graves of the people our family saved."[16]

CHAPTER 16

Humanitarians

February 27 was the first Sunday after Russia's invasion of Ukraine. That day was different at my church, Light Church of Encinitas, California. Our pastor, Benji Horning, shelved his prepared sermon to lead the people in an extended time of prayer for the nation of Ukraine.

For many years Light Church and nearby Faith Community Church of San Diego have partnered to support a children's rescue center and orphanage in Kyiv called Father's House. Pastor Benji shared how at the outbreak of the Russian invasion, the director contacted him about their need to evacuate 150 kids from Father's House and an additional 50 from another orphanage. Father's House needed $32,000 immediately to hire Sprinter vans and buses to evacuate the kids to safety in Poland.

After the funds were sent and received, the director shared a new hurdle: With the flood of people trying to flee Kyiv, no vans or buses were available for hire. Back in San Diego and Encinitas, prayers starting going out about the transportation problem. Shortly after, Benji received a message from the director: "We are not sure how it happened, but we now have two large buses and several smaller vans."

Father's House staff scrambled to get the kids ready, limiting each one to a single school-type backpack. Staff wrote the blood type of each child on a card attached to each pack, in case of wounds or other injuries.

At one point in their journey through active combat zones, one of the buses broke down. Not wanting to leave anyone behind, the entire caravan of buses and vans pulled off to the side of the road. Benji says, "It was an intense situation. It was the middle of the night, and they weren't sure whether Russian forces were nearby. And then after a couple of hours, an empty bus approaches from the opposite direction. The driver stops and says, 'Do you need help? We can leave that bus there, and I can drive you to the border in this one.' So all the kids transfer from the broken bus and off they go. The director wanted to pay the man, but he refused. Later on we tried to contact the bus company and driver, but could not track him down."

Benji pauses and reflects on the event. "Some people would call that [bus arriving] a coincidence. Yeah, you can say whatever you want. I don't care, really, because it's however God wants to do it, you know?"

God's protection surrounded the caravan throughout their entire journey that night. At one point they made a pit stop at a gas station, but just as the kids were filing inside to get a snack and use the restroom, the sound of small arms fire grew closer. The Ukrainian police pulled up as Russian troops were closing in on their position. As the shots grew louder the kids ran from the building back into the buses. The bus drivers were instructed to turn off their headlights and advise everyone to shut down their phones to preserve a blackout.

Sirens blaring, the Ukrainian police escorted the Father's House caravan the rest of the way to the Polish border, even using the opposite side of the highway to avoid a miles-long line of automobiles full of fleeing Ukrainians. Once across the border, the caravan eventually made its way to Freiberg, a German city on the southern edge of the Black Forest.

When Benji asked the Light Church community if any families would be willing to host some of the children, more than one hundred signed up. "The problem is that most of these orphans fled with no paperwork or proper documents, other than perhaps a faded copy of a birth certificate," Benji explains. So the process of getting the children cleared to come to California and be received by host families is on hold—for now. Seven of the older teens in the group, however, do own passports, so hopefully they will soon arrive in San Diego.

In the meantime, the rest of the children in Freiberg settle into a new routine as the older kids attend school, waiting to see what the war will bring. Light Church plans to take groups of people to visit the orphans in Germany and to host children's camps and soccer clinics.

Everywhere I went in Poland and western Ukraine I saw people who want to help, just like Benji Horning back home. Some traveled alone, like Silicon Valley executive search company owner Curt Koland. I met him at the entrance to the humanitarian corridor in Medyka, Poland. Stasz and I had conducted some interviews with aid workers and were leaving to head for our car. As we approached the exit to the corridor I heard an American guy say to a friend, "Let's try to find a ride into town." I stopped and offered them a ride, and we quickly hit it off.

Later that afternoon we sat down in a coffee bar near the lovely old center of Przemyśl, a staging area for humanitarian agencies and workers, located just a few kilometers from the Medyka border crossing. Curt had flown from Bend, Oregon, to Warsaw in early March to help purchase and deliver humanitarian aid. One morning he made his way to one of Warsaw's English-speaking Protestant churches and struck up conversations with folks about the need for aid. "Within minutes I connected with like-minded people who were there to help," he says.

Using his executive skills, Curt quickly procured hundreds of pounds of humanitarian goods and helped get them over the border into Ukraine. He encourages more internationals to come and help. "All you have to do is come, and you will quickly find great needs to be filled. There's much more demand than there is supply."

I heard the same sentiment from Christian Rodriguez, whom I met at a warehouse full of food, water, and other humanitarian supplies in the town of Lublin, Poland. Christian serves as a disaster response manager for Convoy of Hope, a faith-based international nonprofit agency that provides disaster relief in the form of food, supplies, and humanitarian services to needy populations across the globe.

When I spoke to Christian in early April, he said that at that moment, Convoy of Hope was on the ground in twenty-four crisis areas around the world, but that Ukraine was top on their list. Trucks use Poland's large highways like a life-giving bloodstream to transport their materials into Ukraine. Once across the border, they travel Ukraine's smaller arteries to bring the goods to a Lviv warehouse. From there, churches from all across Ukraine retrieve what their cities need and use Ukraine's smaller roads, which vein out into the villages and far-off corners of the country.

At the Operation Blessing tent at the Medyka humanitarian corridor Stasz and I receive a warm welcome from the staff of the Virginia-based nonprofit. We meet Mark Dijkens, originally from the Netherlands, who is the regional director for CBN Europe (the Christian Broadcasting Network). Mark also manages logistics for the Operation Blessing team here in Poland. He knows something about efficiency, having trained and served as a professional butler both in the United States and in the

United Kingdom. "I was a butler for a family near Hartford, England," he says, "when God called me out and said, *Trust Me, I'm going to give you something better.*"

Mark has a big job, but he's confident yet humble about the task ahead. In fact, Operation Blessing—the humanitarian arm of CBN—has been working in Ukraine since 1999. "We are not going anywhere—we will be here at the borders for the long term."

CHAPTER 17

Vasya

My first impression of seventeen-year-old Vasya was completely wrong.

After Stasz and I arrived at the hunting lodge outside Mińsk Mazowiecki, most of the people at the home greeted us with smiles and hugs (see the lodge's story in chapter 3). Vasya, on the other hand, stood about twenty feet away and would only occasionally glance in our direction. He seemed tense and suspicious and kept his distance.

By the end of that first visit he started to talk a little bit, and I found out that he played guitar and was from Vinnytsia, a southwestern Ukrainian city about one hundred kilometers north of the Moldovan border. He had never known his father, and his mother had passed away a few years earlier. Before the war he was living in an orphanage and working at a trade school, where he excelled in metal crafts—using scraps and random pieces of metal to craft artwork.

When Stasz and I returned the next day to do some shopping with the kids, Vasya greeted us with a smile and a handshake.

And the more he opened up, the more I realized how wrong my first impression of him had been.

After dinner that night we had a long talk, and I heard his story. He said, "People wear many faces. Some people have mostly good faces they wear, while other people have bad ones. Sometimes the ones who seem bad are actually good people when they remove their mask."

He went on to talk about the war, and said, "This time of sadness has torn everyone's masks from their faces. The war is allowing us to see people as they really are, good and bad."

I marveled at this wisdom.

When you talk to people who know Vasya, they will confirm that he's not the type of person to wear different faces. "Definitely not," says Bart Sheldrake, who has known Vasya for eleven years. "He's one of the most honest, pure-hearted people I've ever met."

Bart and his wife, Nicole, first met Vasya during Christmas 2011, when Vasya came to Tampa, Florida, to visit via a hosting program. The Sheldrakes were considering adoption and thought the hosting option would be a good way to see if they were meant to adopt. One of Vasya's Christmas gifts was a pack of superhero underwear. When he opened them he was floored. "For me?" he asked. When Bart said yes, they were all his, Vasya started to cry. Back at his orphanage all the boys shared underwear.

"We adored him from the start," says Bart. Other visits followed over the next few years, but due to complications back in Ukraine, Vasya would not become legally adoptable until 2016. In the meantime the Sheldrakes had adopted domestically and were now the proud parents of a son named Noah.

On Vasya's next visit he was a little thrown off that the Sheldrakes had another child. "Do we need to keep him?" Vasya asked.

Bart and Nicole were quick to assure Vasya that he was as much a part of their family as Noah was. "You're my son," Bart would frequently say.

It was hard to see Vasya only once or twice a year—but hosting is expensive, and the family needed to start thinking about saving up for his adoption. "But when we told him that we needed to do fewer hosting visits so we could save for adoption, he was all smiles," Bart says.

In 2014 Nicole gave birth to a son named Luke, which now put Vasya in the role of big brother to two younger siblings. He slowly adjusted to the role as anticipation grew for the time when the wait would be over and he could join his adoptive family in Florida.

Then the Sheldrakes hit another round of snags, including controversy over their marriage certificate, which had been generated in Jamaica, where they had tied the knot. Soon 2016 came and went, and by 2018, it seemed as if a mountain of red tape might forever separate the Sheldrakes from bringing Vasya to America. It was a tough slog the next three years, including during the coronavirus pandemic.

By 2021, however, things began to look up, and the marriage certificate problem—along with other complications on the Ukrainian end—had been solved. With much of the prodigious pile of paperwork now resolved, Bart flew to Kyiv in November 2021 to hand-deliver some key documents. By February 2022, documents completely sorted, the Sheldrakes received their appointment with Ukraine's official adoption office.

Their appointment date was set for February 26, 2022.

On February 24 Bart got the word from the Ukrainian government: "All adoptions have stopped." They were two days short.

As the fog of war descended on Vinnytsia, Bart looked for ways to get to his son. But each time he thought he had found a way, he was held back. Even during those times of uncertainty,

Bart says he felt "a peace that passes all understanding," which is a phrase from the Bible verse Philippians 4:7.

He and Vasya also maintained frequent contact. "Lots of people knock Facebook, but it was a blessing to us. It was our lifeline to Vasya in the early days of the war," Bart says. Father and son connected often, and Bart told Vasya to call him anytime, day or night. "I never put my phone in sleep mode," he adds.

One night Bart was awakened at 2:00 a.m. by the familiar tone of a FaceTime call. It was Vasya. "Dad, I can't sleep. There are explosions very near me."

They later found out that an ammunition depot had been blown up just minutes away. "My heart broke in that call when he told me he was scared," Bart adds.

As the fighting progressed, Vasya wanted to assure his dad that he was okay, no matter what happened. He told Bart, "Dad, I am Ukrainian. I was born here, and if I have to, I will fight and die here."

After holding out in shelters in Vinnytsia for several weeks, Vasya joined up with Natasha Olshanska and traveled with her group through Lviv to eastern Poland, and eventually to the hunting lodge, where I met him. He crossed the border six weeks shy of his eighteenth birthday.

Now that he has turned eighteen, his options have become more open. As an adult, Vasya is not confined to Poland. Nor is he certain about whether he will return to Ukraine.

"We want him here with us," Bart says with no equivocation. "We were two days short . . . I should have been there for him. All the delays and to get that close and then . . . this. Why had I not pushed harder a lot earlier?" Bart says.

But Vasya, ever grace giving, told his dad that it wasn't his fault, and that he's confident they will be together soon. Bart and Nicole are now weighing their options as they explore ways to bring Vasya to the United States.

"We aren't going to give up on our oldest son," Bart says. "After every phone or video call, Vasya always signs off with, 'Be good and I'll see you soon,'" he adds, his voice cracking a bit.

Bart takes the sign-off to heart and believes it will be true.

CHAPTER 18

What Would Christ Have Done?

One of the workers Stasz and I meet at the Operation Blessing tent along the humanitarian corridor in Medyka is a Russian national named Anatoliy (not his real name). He has traveled from St. Petersburg—more than fifteen hundred kilometers away—to help Ukrainians fleeing across the border. The significance of this is not lost on Stasz, whose father was born in Moscow, and who has traveled throughout Belarus and western Russia. Anatoliy had to negotiate checkpoints in Belarus to get across the Polish border.

We ask what it's like for a Russian citizen to come and volunteer at a border crossing being used by hundreds of thousands of Ukrainians fleeing Russian bombs. Anatoliy says, "It's an honor. What my government is doing deeply saddens me, but I am responsible for my own choice. As I prayed about what to do, God clearly told me to come to Poland to help."

When we ask Anatoliy what he will do once the war is over, he doesn't hesitate: "I will go back to my life in St. Petersburg and do what God directs. That is my home."

Back in Moscow, Patriarch Kirill, the leader of the Russian Orthodox Church, has publicly supported—and blessed—the

138

Kremlin's invasion of Ukraine. In early March, hundreds of Russian Orthodox clerics called for an immediate stop to the war in Ukraine, going against their patriarch's outspoken support of it.[1] In fact, since the start of the War in Donbas in 2014, many former Russian Orthodox priests in Ukraine have turned their backs on the patriarchy in Russia.

There are others similar to Anatoliy and the multitudes of Orthodox priests and clerics who have condemned the war. In an April report by the BBC, Father Nicolay Pluzhnik, a Ukrainian priest, said,

> I will never forget the moment when I woke up early to go to mass, only to suddenly hear the shocking sounds of bombing. . . . The wonderful woman who cooked at our church and her son, who was in a wheelchair, were both killed when an artillery shell hit their apartment. I now know of several other of our parishioners who have died.[2]

As a result of what he has witnessed firsthand through the suffering in his own congregation, Father Nicolay has since applied to join the Ukrainian Orthodox Church, which was granted independence from the Russian Orthodox Church in 2019, a move not recognized by Moscow.

These are men and women with strong ties to Russia, but who have decided to stand up to the injustices being committed against the Ukrainian people. Another of them is Russian Orthodox Abbot Daniil Irbits from St. George Monastery in Götschendorf, Germany. He and the monks at the monastery decided to open their doors to more than twenty Ukrainian refugees. It pains him that his patriarch has come out in support of Russia's invasion.

"We have to ask, what would Christ have done? I think Christ would have allowed this," says Father Daniil. He's referring to his decision to give shelter to the Ukrainians under his roof, whom he has integrated into the daily rhythm of the monastery. "In the monastery we live by the principle *Ora et Labora*, Pray and Work," he says. "We have four hectares of land, so there's plenty to do."[3]

One of the sheltered is Ira, who fled Kyiv and is here with her family. As a practicing Christian, she met Father Daniil some time ago through Facebook. When the war broke out, she assumed the abbot would help her, and she was right. "To me, being here is heavenly peace. The nights are quiet, and we hope and know we will wake up every morning."

Ira is on her hands and knees, a garden trowel rhythmically turning the rich garden soil, and she smiles as she works.

CHAPTER 19

Ukraine's Indigenous Peoples

In July 2021 Ukrainian President Volodymyr Zelensky initiated a bill that recognizes three Indigenous people groups. The bill includes Crimean Tatars, along with two Jewish ethno-religious minority groups, the Karaites and Krymchaks, also from Crimea. The bill passed in the Ukrainian Parliament by an overwhelming 94 percent of the deputies who were participants in the voting. [1]

While there are many ethnic minority groups living in Ukraine—including Russians, Poles, Romanians, and Georgians, among others—the significance of the Ukrainian bill is that all three groups recognized are peoples who do not have a state outside the borders of Ukraine.

The Karaites (also known as Karaims) are an autochthonous (meaning "formed in its present position") people of Crimea. Since the eleventh century many have lived in or near Chufut-Kale city-fortress, along the southern coast of Crimea. They are Turkic-speaking observers of Karaite Judaism who do not accept the Talmud and who believe that it is necessary to read the original source and interpret it themselves. It's estimated that only about 2,000 Karaites remain worldwide. [2]

The Krymchaks are an ancient Crimean people who have been on the peninsula since the second century. They practice Orthodox Judaism and speak a varied form of the Crimean Tatar language. Scientists believe that they may be descendants of those Jews who avoided execution during an uprising called the Bar Kokhba Revolt, which took place in the Roman province of Judaea between AD 132–135. Fleeing the armies of Emperor Hadrian, these Jewish refugees made their way to Crimea.[3] It's estimated that there are about 15,000 Krymchaks in the world.

Besides the three groups newly recognized in 2021 (i.e., Krymchaks, Karaites, and Crimean Tatars), there are two other Indigenous groups in Ukraine: ethnic Ukrainians and the Gagauz people, a Turkic-speaking group that practices Eastern Orthodox Christianity. Of the approximately 160,000 Gagauzes, most live in Moldova, while others remain in Ukraine.[4]

Other than Ukrainians themselves, the Crimean Tatars (the third newly recognized group) are by far the largest of the five Indigenous groups in the country, with an estimated 250,000 living in Crimea. These Tatars are a Turkic Muslim people whose roots on the peninsula can be traced back to the thirteenth century.

In many ways the history of Crimea's Tatars reflects the long and complex history between Ukraine and Russia. In 1783 Catherine the Great annexed Crimea, and in the 1850s when Russia eyed expansion of its territory south of the Danube River, the Turks pushed back. The result was the Crimean War, fought by the Ottoman Turks, French, and Sardinians on one side and the Russians on the other. The Russians lost and accused the Crimean Tatars of collusion. As a result, decades of persecution followed.[5]

Nearly one hundred years later the rise of Stalin saw another sharp increase in Russia's persecution of Crimean Tatars. Author and foreign policy analyst Elmira Bayrasli—of Tatar roots herself—points to Stalin's renewal of Russia's centuries-old ambitions in Crimea. She writes that starting in May 1944,

> Stalin then began a more thorough ethnic cleansing of the Tatars, deporting them to the Central Asian state of Uzbekistan. Half died on the journey from disease and starvation, by some estimates. Several thousand Tatars managed to escape to Turkey and into Europe. Some, like my family, ended up in the United States.[6]

In 2015, Ukraine recognized this tragic purge as genocide.

Bayrasli further points out that it wasn't until 1989, under Mikael Gorbachev, that the USSR officially recognized Crimea's Tatars as "a repressed people who were illegally deported."[7] For a period of twenty-five years Tatars began to return to Crimea, and by 2014 their number was estimated at a quarter million—roughly the same number as before Stalin's brutal deportations.

Then came Russia's annexation of Crimea in March 2014, as the world mostly stood by and watched. Uncertainty has once again descended upon Crimea as a whole and upon its Tatar people. Indeed, over the past eight years the cultural détente under Gorbachev has evaporated as the Tatars suffer continuing persecution.

In 2016 the fate of Crimea's Tatars was spotlighted on the world stage by Jamala, a Ukrainian singer whose father is a Crimean Tatar. That year she won the Eurovision Song Contest with her song "1944," which highlights the sad history of the Soviet deportation of the Tatars. In March 2022, having fled Ukraine two weeks earlier, Jamala reprised the song during the Concert for Ukraine held in Birmingham, United Kingdom. The concert—which also featured performances by Ed Sheeran, Camila Cabello, and Snow Patrol—raised money for Ukrainian humanitarian aid efforts.[8]

In response to Russia's 2014 illegal seizure of Crimea, many Tatars decided to take up arms. In 2014 Crimean Tatar Isa Akayev (not his real name) managed to escape Crimea and move to Vinnytsia, Ukraine.[9] But he could not simply stand by and watch. In response, he formed the Crimea Regiment, a fighting force of Crimean Tatars who saw action in the War in Donbas.

In late February 2022 the mostly Muslim soldiers of the Crimea Regiment saw intense action in the battle for Kyiv. Akayev and his men were among the first Ukrainian fighters inside the village of Motyzhyn after Russian forces were repelled in that battle (see "Maksym and Roksolana," chapter 9). He and his men discovered shallow graves containing dead civilians in the woods. As he walks among the horrific scene, he says, "They were a woman, her husband, and a kid. Such a sick thing to do . . . I firmly believe I'll fight until the bitter end."[10]

Ukraine is a varied, complex nation with a wide array of cultural, ethnic, religious, and political views and people groups. Akayev says he is fighting for the same thing as his fellow Ukrainians of every faith background: the freedom of his nation and the restoration of peace. "I realize that what we are doing now will lead us to Crimea and to the liberation of all other territories occupied by Russia."[11]

Crimea remains a microcosm of Ukraine—a place where Christians, Jews, and Muslims find themselves galvanized by a common goal of self-preservation, religious freedom, and national sovereignty.

CHAPTER 20

Should We Love Our Enemies?

A 2018 Pew Research poll revealed that nearly 90 percent of Americans believe in some kind of higher power. Just over half—56 percent—say they believe in "God as described in the Bible," while nearly 33 percent say they believe in "another type of higher power or spiritual force."[1] So while most of us believe in the existence of God, the conversation grows more divisive when you pose this question:

If God loves and cares about us,
why does He allow bad things to happen in the world?

As a Christian who falls into the 56 percent bucket, it's a question I asked God when, in 2001, my wife and I lost our three-day-old son, Joseph, to a rare genetic disorder. I learned too well the painful truth of the adage that "no parent should have to bury their child."

The older I get, however, the more I believe God's shoulders are quite broad. As my dad used to say, "God isn't falling off His throne when we ask the tough questions." I think it's healthy—and potentially faith expanding—to wrestle with questions of evil and death.

The shortest verse in the Bible reveals a profound truth: "Jesus wept" (John 11:35). This verse describes His response at hearing the news that His friend Lazarus had died. But here's the thing: Jesus was already on His way to heal Lazarus, so wouldn't He have been calm and confident, knowing the positive future outcome? It suggests that Jesus was not weeping for Lazarus, but out of compassion for those who were mourning him. And perhaps Jesus, being only a few days away from the crucifixion, was mourning the cost He would have to pay for Lazarus's resurrection—and His own. Lastly, Jesus knew that raising Lazarus from the dead could fuel the final accusations the Pharisees needed to put Him on the cross.

In the story of Lazarus, we see a Jesus who loves deeply and compassionately. Jesus' last words before His death on the cross were in the form of a question. When God turned away from His Son as Jesus took on the sins of the world, Jesus asked, "Eloi, Eloi, lama sabachthani?" or "My God, my God, why have you forsaken me?" (Matthew 27:46).

Yes, Jesus was suffering terribly, and yes, God turned away when Jesus took on the sins of the world as a sacrifice for us. However, there's another deeper purpose here. Jesus was quoting Psalm 22, a psalm written by David nearly a thousand years earlier. It's a prophetic psalm that points toward the future Messiah, and it talks about how the clothing of the subject was divided up and the oppressors "cast lots" for it (verse 18). I believe this prophecy was fulfilled at the cross when soldiers cast lots—gambled—to see who would win Jesus' garments (see Matthew 27:35).

Psalm 22 is bursting with prophetic signposts pointing to the Messiah. The main point is that Jesus was quoting a psalm that God's chosen people, the Jews, would be very familiar with. The words were spoken in Aramaic, the common language (along with Hebrew), and they were spoken to Jews well-versed in the Torah who would immediately grasp the inference to Psalm 22. Even in His last breaths from the cross, Jesus implores His fellow Jews to embrace the Messiah. "Eloi, Eloi, lama sabachthani?" were not (only) words of anguish spoken to a God who had turned His face, but words spoken as a prompt to the people of Israel, for whom Jesus mourned.

Even in His darkest hour, we see a Jesus who loves deeply and compassionately.

When it comes to the question of how a good God could allow so much bad in the world, pat answers fall flat for many of us. What I have learned, though, is that God has been there for me despite the bad—irrespective of evil. I have learned that it can be beneficial to question and probe God, especially if such questioning deepens our understanding of a God who loved us so much that He sacrificed His Son to pay for our sins. For as we grow, and as we experience the reality of God's love in the midst of our suffering, it breaks us open so that His love can pour through us to water a thirsty world.

I believe free will exists in the world, and God loves and esteems us enough to grant us the liberty to make our own choices. Both good and bad choices are made by both good and bad people. King David is a popular example. I believe God's grace and salvation are free (because Jesus already paid the ransom price for us), but I also believe faith is a choice that grows in proportion to one's commitment and ability to honor that choice. Like marital fidelity or unconditional love, if faith weren't a choice, what would be its value?

Along with this compelling question of God's love in a world full of evil, a second question arises:

Should we love our enemies even during times of war?

As I dove into the research underlying this book, time and again I was confronted by the evil of a war that previously would have seemed implausible in twenty-first-century Europe. But then again, we see such evil abound in nations like Syria, where civilian deaths and atrocities not dissimilar to those taking place in Ukraine have been happening for more than a decade now. (Not coincidentally, the Russian military has been a bad actor in that situation as well.)

It does not take long to think of other examples: the slaughter of more than 800,000 Tutsis at the hands of ethnic Hutu extremists in the 1994 Rwandan genocide; Kony's Lord's Resistance Army extant in South Sudan; ISIS in Iraq and the Levant; the Khmer Rouge in Cambodia; the Holocaust and the extermination of more than 6 million Jews; 20 million deaths under Stalin's regime.[2] The list is seemingly endless as we mentally flip back through the decades and centuries.

To wade deeper into such waters I turned to renowned theologian and bestselling author Dr. Michael L. Brown. With a Ph.D. from New York University in Near Eastern languages and literatures, Dr. Brown is recognized as one of the leading Messianic Jewish scholars in the world today.[3] He also hosts the nationally syndicated daily talk radio show *The Line of Fire* and has authored more than forty books. I've been honored to edit and help publish three of Michael's books, and am privileged to count him as a friend. The rest of this chapter is from a piece he wrote in April 2022 that helps answers that question, *Should we love our enemies even during times of war?*

> Recently, some Christians in Ukraine came under fire for putting up billboards in their city with verses from the Bible, one of which quoted the words of Jesus from the Sermon on the Mount where He called us to love our enemies (see Matthew 5:43–48). As a result, these Christians have been branded separatists and traitors, with some calling for their church to be investigated.

But was Jesus referring to situations like this when He called us to love our enemies? Are we to love those who ruthlessly bomb our families? Are we to love those who rape our women and murder our children? Are we to love those who tie the hands of civilians behind their backs before executing them? Is this really what Jesus meant?

To be sure, these Ukrainian Christians (some of whom I know) were not calling for pacifism. They believe in defending their country, and they believe in the use of force to resist and repel the attack on their nation. In fact, I could easily see them praying for God to be with them as they fought against the Russian army, the result of which would be Russian casualties.

That is how you can love your enemies even during a time of war, all while fighting with all your might to defeat that very enemy.

But can you love an enemy soldier while at the same time trying to kill him before he kills you?

Let's first consider whom Jesus was talking to in the Sermon on the Mount, namely, first-century Jews under the occupation of Rome. They had personal enemies, religious enemies, and national enemies. And there were some Jewish groups who taught that it was absolutely right to hate their enemies.

Jesus says absolutely not. We are to love them, even the worst of them.

How Do You Love Your Enemy in Times of War?

That means that, in times of war, you would rather see your enemy surrender than kill him, and if he did surrender, you would not treat him harshly.

It means that you would recognize his humanity, remembering that he has a loving wife and children (or parents) waiting for him at home.

That you would understand that, in all likelihood, he is simply following orders and has been fed lots of misinformation about you.

That you would want to see him rehabilitated after the war, truly repenting for his actions, truly coming to know God, and living a redemptive life. (In the case of someone who committed war crimes and would be sentenced to prison or death, even then, you would want him to repent and get right with God before he died.)

That you would even have pity on the enemy who has seemingly lost all human feeling to the point of acting like a rabid animal. Surely this was not who God created him to be. Even if he must die, we should pity his poor, lost soul.

That is how you can love your enemies even during a time of war, all while fighting with all your might to defeat that very enemy.

Seeing the Humanity of Our Enemy

Some might quip in facetious response, "So, it looks like this? Before the sniper shoots the enemy in the head, he mutters under his breath, 'Jesus loves you, and so do I. Here's a token of my love. Bang!'"

Obviously not.

But he might pray regularly for God to have mercy on those he has to take out. Or for God to help the widows and orphans left behind. Or for God to give them a change of heart and mind, resulting in a change of actions, so the sniper does not need to take them out.

On the other hand, if the sniper enjoys the kill itself, if he revels in the bloodshed and longs to have the opportunity to take more enemy lives, I would question how much of the love of God is in his heart.

The fact is that we are products of our environment more than we care to realize, and the ones we brand as terrorists are often hailed as freedom fighters by their people. (Ask yourself this: How would British historians writing in the early 1800s describe the Revolutionary War? Our American heroes and freedom fighters were anything but that in their eyes.)

And are all Russians guilty of the barbaric Ukraine invasion? Should all Russians be blamed and hated? Obviously not.

Of course, I'm not saying there is no such thing as objective morality. Quite the contrary. For example, there was nothing good or noble about the Nazi cause. It was downright evil, to the core. And the Nazis absolutely deserved what they got. I wish they had been stopped in their tracks and destroyed years earlier.

Forgiving Our Enemy

Yet, as New Testament scholar Craig Keener notes in his shorter Matthew commentary, Jesus

> also makes a demand that can require more than merely human resources for forgiveness. Corrie ten Boom, who had lost most of her family in a Nazi concentration camp, often lectured on grace. But one day a man who came to shake her hand after such a talk turned out to be a former prison guard. Only by asking God to love through her did she find the grace to take his hand and offer him Christian forgiveness.[4]

So, by all legal means, let the Ukrainians fight against the Russian invaders, and may their triumph over the Russian army put a stop to this senseless shedding of blood. And may the Ukrainian Christians continue to love their enemies through it all. (For those of us feeling smugly self-righteous right now, how about *us* loving *our* enemies, right where we live?)

CHAPTER 21

A Spiritual Perspective on the War

*W*e asked respected prophetic voice and bestselling author Chuck D. Pierce to give an analysis of the war in Ukraine from a spiritual perspective. Pierce is president of Glory of Zion International Ministries (www.gloryofzion .org) and also president of Global Spheres, Inc. in Corinth, Texas. His story follows.*

What we are seeing in Ukraine right now is not only the largest military conflict in Europe since World War II, but a major spiritual battle that has critical implications for the Church around the globe.

I visited Ukraine in 2004 and 2008 to meet with leaders and talk about how there would be conflict in days ahead. Six years before Russia annexed Crimea and helped foment the War in Donbas, I shared how Russia would return to try to take back one of the breadbaskets of the world.

We are seeing this now in the Black Sea as Russia's navy has cut off seaport shipments of key products from Ukraine, including their critical grain harvests. Additionally, Russia has stolen hundreds of tons of Ukrainian grain. The effects of the war are already hurting the poorest areas of the world, particularly Africa. The impact is great because Ukraine is one of the world's largest suppliers of wheat, accounting for nearly 12 percent of the global supply and 17 percent of the world's corn.[1]

When Putin sent his troops across the border into Ukraine in early 2022, it further confirmed that we are not only witnessing an unprecedented military invasion, but a massive spiritual conflict as well. And the attack on Ukraine—both militarily and spiritually—is a critical part of a larger conflict. Specifically, I believe we are in the midst of a seven-year war that has global spiritual, geopolitical, and military implications.

In late summer 2019, I received a prophetic word saying that the Church was entering a period of intense conflict, starting with "plague-like conditions" that would hit the world by Passover 2020 (what turned out to be the coronavirus pandemic, which began a few months before Passover that year). God impressed on me that this seven-year war would culminate in 2026, and that it would unfold in the natural world through an epic power struggle between the United States, China, and Russia. He further told me that this power move would involve key ports and entry points around the world (e.g., Russia's Black Sea blockade, as mentioned above). I write about these factors in my 2020 book *The Passover Prophecies.*

We are in the middle part of this seven-year spiritual war. We are in an acutely critical time in the history of God's Church, as we must leave behind any complacency or "business as usual" approaches to prayer. God is looking for a remnant that will stand in the gap for spiritual hot spots such as Ukraine. God's church has been asleep, particularly in the West, and the Russian invasion of Ukraine is a resounding wake-up call.

This invasion by Russia is not just about that nation's military objectives. We are experiencing a major battle being fought in the spiritual realm, whereby the enemy is attempting to bring chaos, disorder, and economic upheaval on a global scale.

I believe a key word for our present time is the Hebrew word for Passover, which is *pesach*. This word means "to pass over or protect." In Exodus 12, the Spirit of God "passes over" the homes of the Hebrews in captivity whose door frames were marked by the blood of the lamb. Similarly today, God is looking for those who are marked by the blood of the Lamb—Christ Jesus—and for His remnant to stand up and fight in the power of the Holy Spirit.

The following is an excerpt from *The Passover Prophecies* that has keen relevance for the current state of the world.

> Every Passover has economic ramifications. The plague-like conditions that I was foreseeing late summer 2019 were actually not the most alarming aspect of what God was speaking to me. Rather, my greatest motivation was understanding the *economic ramifications* of these conditions. As I studied and researched, I first looked biblically at the economic models that occurred during Passover throughout the Word of God.
>
> For instance, the favor the Hebrews enjoyed during the lifetime of Joseph ended when he and his brothers passed away. Though the Hebrews continued to grow in strength and number, a new Pharaoh came to power, and with him came a reversal of favor and fortune. The Hebrews were enslaved, and their economic livelihood was stripped away. In fact, their very future as a people was in jeopardy as this unforgiving Pharaoh ordered the Egyptian midwives to kill every newborn male child born to a Hebrew woman. (See Exodus 1.)[2]

Similarly today, we see a Pharoah-like nation killing innocent children in an unprovoked and brutal war. While few of us are called to fight militarily on behalf of the sovereignty of the nation of Ukraine, we can all fight in the spiritual realm. And just as in the time of Pharoah in the book of Exodus, we are also seeing the economic ramifications of a superpower's lust for land and subjugation of a people.

In *The Passover Prophecies* I further write,

> In the same way that God needed to prepare the Israelites to cross over and begin to walk into their inheritance, God is circumcising our hearts as a church—stripping us of the things of our past that might block our ability to "pass over" into this new season. . . .
>
> Remember, Egypt was a worldly economic power structure that was *not* moving in God's purposes—just the opposite. Today we are dealing with similar "Pharaoh-like" economic and military power structures in the world.[3]

If we allow God to circumcise our hearts and prepare us for battle, just as He did with the Israelites before the battle of Jericho, I firmly believe that the tide can be turned and this seven-year spiritual war can be won. What is manifesting in Ukraine is just one global event among many.

Since 1986 I have had a deep interest in China, and have prayed for that nation continuously. Millions of people have come to Christ in China, particularly over the past thirty years, and God is moving powerfully there. But at the same time, China must be watched closely in the coming days and months. Just as Russia has showed its hand in its unprovoked attack on Ukraine, China has its eyes on places like Taiwan.

Again, as God's Church we play a vital role through the ministry of prayer and intercession. The time is now for a global army to rise up and stand in the gap for the purposes of God on the earth. The war is underway. There is absolutely no time to waste.

CHAPTER 22

Do, Go

One evening in early April 2022, back in our hostel in Przemyśl, Poland, I stumbled on a blog post on the website of the *London Review of Books*. It caught my eye because the title was "In Przemyśl," which is where I was at the time. The author had just returned from several weeks volunteering at the Medyka border crossing, where we had spent the last couple of days.

This author speaks English and Russian and had been using her language skills to direct displaced Ukrainians and help in other ways. She was frustrated, however, with the number of monolingual American and Western volunteers who had shown up at the borders to help. She wrote, "I wonder what has made them come all this way instead of donating the hundreds of pounds it has cost them to one of the relief funds. What do they have to offer that is worth their taking up a bed desperately needed by a displaced person?"[1]

The writer makes some great points, and I agree that it would have been far better initially for volunteers to stay farther afield than to take up much-needed beds near the border.

And admittedly, in the month of March, the tide of Ukrainians flowing across the border into Poland was staggering. Some people I spoke with before I wrote these stories waited between eighteen and thirty hours to cross. And then once across, for many there was an immediate need for temporary housing.

By the time Stasz and I arrived in Przemyśl, however, the tide had slowed somewhat. Still, we were careful to pick a hostel that had both men's and women's wings—the women's wing was about two-thirds full of Ukrainian women, while the men's side was empty except for us. Since March the flow of Ukrainians has slowed (but certainly not stopped), and most Ukrainians who wanted—or needed—to leave, have. So this is what I have to say to anyone—even if your only language is English—who may feel led to go to Eastern Europe to volunteer:

Go.

As I often heard, the demands far outstrip the supply of aid and resources the Ukrainians need, and their needs are not dissipating any time soon. Also, at this point in the war, the primary need along the eastern borders of nations such as Poland has shifted from transport and housing (helping with the critical and immediate needs of border crossers) to aid provision. None of us know how long this war will drag on. As I write this, analysts are projecting a slow, bruising conflict that could last months, if not years. God willing, by the time you are reading this the war may be over.

But even so, the road to recovery for Ukraine is going to be long and hard. Consider how you can best invest your time, talents, and treasure to help postwar Ukraine. Some of us are called to go, while some of us can do significant work right where we are. Whatever the case, *do* or *go*. Think about and pray for ways you can help.

The Ukrainian people will be forever grateful.

Notes

Chapter 4 At the Gates of Mariupol

1. "The Siege of Mariupol," France 24, August 5, 2022, https://www.france 24.com/en/live-news/20220508-the-siege-of-mariupol.

2. Mark Kramer, "Why Did Russia Give Away Crimea Sixty Years Ago?" The Wilson Center, accessed June 3, 2022, https://www.wilsoncenter.org /publication/why-did-russia-give-away-crimea-sixty-years-ago.

3. Kramer, "Why Did Russia Give Away Crimea."

4. RFE/RL's Ukrainian Service, "British Investigators: More Evidence Found of Russian Role in Donbas," RadioFreeEurope RadioLiberty, August 19, 2019, https://www.rferl.org/a/british-online-research-group-says-more -evidence-found-of-russian-role-in-donbas-conflict/30116665.html.

5. Office of the United Nations High Commissioner for Human Rights, Conflict-Related Civilian Casualties in Ukraine (January 27, 2022), https:// ukraine.un.org/en/download/96187/168060.

Chapter 6 Exploited

1. Amanda Buenger, "Team 3: Update from Ukrainian Response," Unbound Now, April 15, 2022, https://www.unboundnow.org/blog/team-3-update -from-ukrainian-response.

2. Home page, Unbound Now, accessed June 7, 2022, https://www.un boundnow.org.

3. Michael Birnbaum and Mary Ilyushina, "Ukrainian Refugees in Russia Report Interrogations, Detention and Other Abuses," *Washington Post*, May 11, 2022, https://www.washingtonpost.com/world/2022/05/11/ukraine -refugees-russia-filtration-camps.

4. Sophie Ankel, "The Kremlin Plans to Send 100,000 Ukrainians to Siberia and the Arctic Circle, Report Says, as Zelenskyy Warns of 'Filtration Camps' for Captured People," Insider, April 12, 2022, https://www.business insider.com/russia-plans-to-send-ukrainians-to-siberia-arctic-circle-report -2022-4.

5. "Ambassador Thomas-Greenfield on the Humanitarian Impact of Russia's War against Ukraine," U.S. Embassy in Chile, April 5, 2022, https://cl .usembassy.gov/ambassador-thomas-greenfield-on-the-humanitarian-impact -of-russias-war-against-ukraine.

6. Associated Press and Chris Pleasance, "More Than 400,000 Ukrainians Including 84,000 Children Have Been Abducted and Taken to Russian Cities and May Be Used as 'Hostages' to Force a Surrender, Kyiv Warns," *Daily Mail*, March 25, 2022, https://www.dailymail.co.uk/news/article-10646603 /Ukraine-president-pleads-worldwide-support.html.

Chapter 9 Maksym and Roksolana

1. "Ukraine 'Road of Death' Shows Russians Fired on Civilians: A Video Investigation," *Wall Street Journal*, May 12, 2022, https://on.wsj.com/3l4icsi.

Chapter 10 The Vest

1. Stuart Ramsay, "Sky News Team's Harrowing Account of Their Violent Ambush in Ukraine This Week," Sky News, March 5, 2022, https://news.sky .com/story/sky-news-teams-harrowing-account-of-their-violent-ambush-in -ukraine-this-week-12557585.

2. Roshni Ravi, "Body Armor for Ukraine," Body Armor News, March 17, 2022, https://www.bodyarmornews.com/body-armor-for-ukraine.

Chapter 11 Gennadiy Mokhnenko

1. "Ukrainians to Be Proud of: Gennadiy Mokhnenko—Pastor of a Protestant Church, Military Chaplain and Father of 38 Kids," Republic Pilgrim, accessed June 6, 2022, https://republicpilgrim.org/en/ukrainians-to-be-proud -of-gennadiy-mokhnenko-pastor-father-of-38-kids.

2. "Gennadiy Mokhnenko."

3. "Gennadiy Mokhnenko."

4. "Russians, Don't Be Fooled by the Madness of the Kremlin Scoundrels, Don't Send Your Children to the Meat Grinder—Pastor Gennadiy Mokhnenko" (accompanying video), Religious Information Service of Ukraine, February 21, 2022, https://risu.ua/en/russians-dont-be-fooled-by-the-madness -of-the-kremlin-scoundrels-dont-send-your-children-to-the-meat-grinder ---pastor-gennadiy-mokhnenko_n126273.

5. "A World Without Orphans Bike Tour 2017," World Without Orphans, last modified August 2, 2017, https://worldwithoutorphans.org/story/a-world -without-orphans-bike-tour-2017.

6. "Ukraine: Children without Caregivers Risk Being Forgotten," Save the Children, March 14, 2022, https://www.savethechildren.net/news/ukraine-children-without-caregivers-risk-being-forgotten.

7. "The Charity Fund 'Pilgrim,'" About Us, Republic Pilgrim, accessed June 6, 2022, https://republicpilgrim.org/en/about-us.

8. *Almost Holy*, directed by Steve Hoover (Animal, 2016), 1:36:32. https://www.youtube.com/watch?v=QHvMLQ-LCV0.

9. "Russians, Don't Be Fooled."

10. "Russians, Don't Be Fooled."

11. Serving Orphans Worldwide, "Our field coordinator, Coleman Bailey is with Pastor Gennadiy Mokhnenko in Eastern Ukraine," Facebook video, March 24, 2022, https://www.facebook.com/watch/?v=1007976530126562.

12. Serving Orphans Worldwide, "CNN Interviews Pastor Gennadiy," Facebook video, April 7, 2022, https://www.facebook.com/watch/?v=1078870423047081.

13. Serving Orphans Worldwide, "CNN Interviews Pastor Gennadiy."

Chapter 12 Jhenya

1. "Somerset Maugham on Love, Duty and Free Will," Mockingbird, last modified November 10, 2010, https://mbird.com/literature/love-and-duty-in-painted-veil.

2. Although this quote is frequently attributed to C. S. Lewis, it's questionable whether he actually said or wrote it. See William O'Flaherty, "Experience That Most Brutal," Essential C.S. Lewis, September 12, 2015, updated June 9, 2018, https://essentialcslewis.com/2015/09/12/experience-that-most-brutal.

Chapter 13 Colonel Korenevych

1. Editorial Board, "Ronald Reagan and the Power to Change History," *Washington Post*, June 7, 2012, https://www.washingtonpost.com/opinions/ronald-reagan-and-the-power-to-change-history/2012/06/07/gJQAQI9VLV_story.html.

Chapter 15 Ukraine's Deep Jewish Roots

1. Jennifer Popowycz, "The 'Holocaust by Bullets' in Ukraine," National WWII Museum, January 24, 2022, https://www.nationalww2museum.org/war/articles/ukraine-holocaust.

2. Popowycz, "Holocaust by Bullets."

3. Dan Ben-Amos, "Israel ben Eliezer, the Baal Shem Tov," in *Judaism in Practice*, ed. Lawrence Fine (Princeton: Princeton University Press, 2001), 498–512, https://repository.upenn.edu/cgi/viewcontent.cgi?article=1126&context=nelc_papers.

4. Matthew Kupfer, "5 Books with Insight into Ukrainian-Jewish History," *Kyiv Post*, May 9, 2019, https://www.kyivpost.com/business/5-books-with -insight-into-ukrainian-jewish-history.html.

5. David Lepeska, "Ukraine Embraces Its Jewish Minority, and Reckons with Its Traumatic History," New Lines Magazine, October 13, 2021, https:// newlinesmag.com/essays/ukraine-embraces-its-jewish-minority-and-reckons -with-its-traumatic-history.

6. United States Holocaust Memorial Museum, "Pogroms," Holocaust Encyclopedia, accessed on June 6, 2022, https://encyclopedia.ushmm.org /content/en/article/pogroms.

7. Jeffrey Veidlinger, "The Killing Fields of Ukraine," Tablet, February 22, 2022, https://www.tabletmag.com/sections/history/articles/killing-fields -ukraine.

8. Popowycz, "Holocaust by Bullets."

9. Cnaan Liphshiz, "Russian Bombs Appear to Hit Site of Babyn Yar Nazi Massacre near Kyiv," Jewish Telegraphic Agency, March 1, 2022, https:// www.jta.org/2022/03/01/global/russian-bombs-appear-to-hit-site-of-babyn -yar-nazi-massacre-near-kyiv.

10. Gillian Brockell, "Putin Says He'll 'Denazify' Ukraine. Its Jewish President Lost Family in the Holocaust," *Washington Post,* February 25, 2022, https://www.washingtonpost.com/history/2022/02/25/zelensky-family -jewish-holocaust.

11. Brockell, "Putin Says He'll 'Denazify' Ukraine."

12. Brockell, "Putin Says He'll 'Denazify' Ukraine."

13. "Names of Righteous by Country," Yad Vashem, last modified January 1, 2021, https://www.yadvashem.org/righteous/statistics.html.

14. Stewart Ain, "15 'Righteous Gentiles' Lived in Ukraine," Jewish Standard, May 18, 2022, https://jewishstandard.timesofisrael.com/15-righteous -gentiles-lived-in-ukraine.

15. Ain, "15 'Righteous Gentiles.'"

16. Ain, "15 'Righteous Gentiles.'"

Chapter 18 What Would Christ Have Done?

1. Idel.Realities, "Orthodox Deacon Who Called for End to War in Ukraine Flees Russia," Radio Free Europe / RadioLiberty, April 12, 2022, https:// www.rferl.org/a/russia-deacon-flees-ukraine-war/31798820.html.

2. Nicolay Pluzhnik, "'I'm Shocked by My Church Leaders in Moscow'— Priest in Ukraine," interview by Aleem Maqbool, BBC News, April 15, 2022, https://www.bbc.com/news/world-europe-61109104.

3. DW News, "Russian Orthodox Monks Take in Ukrainian Refugees in Germany," filmed at St. George Russian Orthodox monastery in Germany, posted April 23, 2022, video, 5:05, https://www.youtube.com/watch?v=OU 9UGxzw9JQ.

Chapter 19 Ukraine's Indigenous Peoples

1. Ali Cura and Emre Gürkan Abay, "Ukraine's Parliament Adopts Law on Indigenous Peoples," Anadolu Agency, February 7, 2021, https://www.aa .com.tr/en/europe/ukraine-s-parliament-adopts-law-on-indigenous-peoples /2291885.

2. Tetyana Matychak, "Indigenous Peoples in Ukraine You May Have Never Heard About," Ukraine World, July 23, 2019, https://ukraineworld .org/articles/opinions/indigenous-peoples-ukraine-you-may-have-never -heard-about.

3. Matychak, "Indigenous Peoples in Ukraine."

4. Matychak, "Indigenous Peoples in Ukraine."

5. Elmira Bayrasli, "Who Will Speak for the Tatars?" Foreign Policy, May 18, 2019, https://foreignpolicy.com/2019/05/18/crimean-tatars-ethnic-cleansing.

6. Bayrasli, "Who Will Speak for the Tatars?"

7. Bayrasli, "Who Will Speak for the Tatars?"

8. Fred Sahai, "Eurovision Winner Jamala Delivers Powerful Performance for Her Home County on 'Concert for Ukraine,'" *Billboard*, March 29, 2022, https://www.billboard.com/music/concerts/ukraine-eurovision-winner -jamala-concert-for-ukraine-video-1235051143.

9. Irenaeus, "Crimean Tatars Join Fellow Ukrainians in the Fight," Daily Kos, March 1, 2022, https://www.dailykos.com/stories/2022/3/1/2083097 /-Crimean-Tatars-Join-Fellow-Ukrainians-in-the-Fight.

10. Al Jazeera, "These Muslim Tatars Are Fighting Russian Soldiers in Ukraine," video, 9:07, https://www.youtube.com/watch?v=8ALTEhcej1E&t =12s.

11. Al Jazeera, "Fighting Russian Soldiers."

Chapter 20 Should We Love Our Enemies?

1. Dalia Fahmy, "Key Findings about Americans' Belief in God," Pew Research Center, April 25, 2018, https://www.pewresearch.org/fact-tank/2018 /04/25/key-findings-about-americans-belief-in-god.

2. Bill Keller, "Major Soviet Paper Says 20 Million Died as Victims of Sta-lin," *New York Times*, February 4, 1989, https://www.nytimes.com/1989/02 /04/world/major-soviet-paper-says-20-million-died-as-victims-of-stalin.html.

3. To find out more about Dr. Brown, visit www.askdrbrown.org.

4. Michael Brown, "Should We Love Our Enemies Even During a Time of War?" Stream, April 19, 2022, https://stream.org/should-we-love-our-enemies -even-during-a-time-of-war.

Chapter 21 A Spiritual Perspective on the War

1. John Reidy, "Ukraine Unable to Move Grain to Markets," World-Grain .com, last modified May 4, 2022, https://www.world-grain.com/articles/16857 -ukraine-unable-to-move-grain-to-markets.

2. Chuck D. Pierce, *The Passover Prophecies: How God Is Realigning Hearts and Nations in Crisis* (Lake Mary, Fla.: Charisma House, 2020), 5–6.
3. Pierce, *Passover Prophecies*, 6–7.

Chapter 22 Do, Go

1. Ada Wordsworth, "In Przemyśl," *London Review of Books*, March 30, 2022, https://www.lrb.co.uk/blog/2022/march/in-przemysl.

Resources

Further information about organizations mentioned in this book

Ukrainian-run organizations assisting the country's soldiers, citizens, and orphans

Father's House

A Kyiv-based charitable organization that responds to the needs of orphans and children at risk in Ukraine. They run a series of programs designed to create a path to societal integration for children of all ages. Reach them at o-dim.com/en.

Johnny and Ira Semeniuk

The Semeniuks are on the ground in Poland making regular aid relief deliveries across the border into Ukraine to assist those affected by the war, including Ukraine's soldiers. Contact them or make a donation at facebook.com/ira.semeniuk.

Olive Branch Ukraine

Headed by former Ukrainian Army Colonel Valentyn Korenevych, Olive Branch works with Ukraine's war chaplains to provide emotional, mental, and spiritual support for Ukraine's fighting men and women. Make a donation or learn more at olivebranch.org.ua/en, or contact them at olivebranch.ua@gmail.com.

Republic Pilgrim

The largest youth recovery center in Eastern Europe, Republic Pilgrim and its founder Gennadiy Mokhnenko are centered in the Donbas warzone areas of Ukraine, providing evacuations for Ukrainian refugees and help for orphans, as well as meeting physical and spiritual needs of Ukraine's military men and women. Learn more or make a donation at republicpilgrim.org/en.

Organizations assisting Ukraine's youth, orphans, and children

International Host Connection

An orphan-hosting organization that helps American and Canadian adults explore the possibilities of hosting orphans in their homes over Christmas and summer vacation. You can reach them via Tasha Bradley at internationalhostconnection.com.

Serving Orphans Worldwide

An orphan-care nonprofit that strives to rescue, train, and sustain struggling children's homes and orphanages in Ukraine and around the world. Reach them at soworldwide.org.

World Without Orphans

A Christian nonprofit organization that calls and equips national leaders to collaborate in solving their own country's orphaned and vulnerable children's crises. Reach them at worldwithout orphans.org.

Youth With A Mission

One of the world's largest Christian youth organizations, YWAM has ministries that cover every sphere of society, including ship-based medical care, performing arts teams, Bible-training programs, business coaching, sports ministries, anti-trafficking work, and many more. Reach them at ywam.org.

Humanitarian and aid relief agencies working in Ukraine

Convoy of Hope

An American nonprofit humanitarian and disaster relief organization that provides food, supplies, and humanitarian services to impoverished or otherwise needy populations throughout the world. They are working actively on the ground in Ukraine. Reach them at convoyofhope.org.

Operation Blessing

A nonprofit humanitarian organization founded in the United States. It is working on the ground in Ukraine to bring relief and aid to the nation. Reach them at ob.org.

Operation Mobilisation

A Christian missionary organization that spreads the love of Christ through church planting, evangelism, relief and development, justice, and mentoring and discipleship. They are actively working to assist Ukrainian refugees as they transit from Ukraine into neighboring allied countries. Reach them at om.org.

Samaritan's Purse

A Christian humanitarian aid organization that provides aid to people in physical need as a key part of its Christian missionary work. They are actively working on the ground in Ukraine. Reach them at samaritanspurse.org.

UNICEF

An agency of the United Nations responsible for providing humanitarian and developmental aid to children worldwide. Reach them at unicefusa.org.

World Central Kitchen

WCK serves meals to disaster- and war-struck areas around the world. They are on the ground on both sides of the border providing hearty meals to Ukrainians. Reach them at wck.org.

World Vision

A global Christian humanitarian organization that partners with children, families, and their communities to reach their full potential by tackling the causes of poverty and injustice. Reach them at worldvision.org.

Anti-human-trafficking and anti-sex-trafficking organizations working in and around Ukraine

Unbound Now

An international anti-sex-trafficking organization based in Texas. They have worked on both sides of the border to thwart the sex traffickers who have descended on the Polish-Ukrainian border. Reach them at unboundnow.org or 855-450-2344.

Global Alliance Against Traffic in Women

An alliance of more than eighty nongovernmental organizations from Africa, Asia, Europe, Latin America and the Caribbean, and North America. Reach them at gaatw.org.

Exodus Cry

An international organization committed to abolishing sex trafficking and breaking the cycle of commercial sexual exploitation while assisting and empowering its victims. Reach them at exoduscry.com.

Kyle Duncan has enjoyed a career in the publishing industry that has spanned nearly four decades. For twenty-five years he served as an editorial executive at several publishing houses where he helped develop nearly 1,500 books, including several million-plus sellers. The native Californian has worked closely with many bestselling authors, including John Wooden, Toby-Mac, Dr. Gary Chapman, and Voice of the Martyrs.

While Kyle was studying English literature at UCLA, a friend told him that the *Daily Bruin* was looking for music critics—which meant free concert tickets. Kyle quickly developed a knack for personal profiles and while still an undergrad sold his first article to *Los Angeles* magazine. Raised in an artistic family, Kyle considered careers in acting (his father, Kirk Duncan, worked in films with Rock Hudson, Gregory Peck, and Gene Hackman) and music production (he interned for IRS Records and Universal Music Group) before setting his sights on publishing.

For the past ten years Kyle has worked as a writing Sherpa and *New York Times* bestselling ghostwriter, helping authors craft their best messages. *Hope for Ukraine* is Kyle's first book and was inspired by his personal experience of adopting his son Cory "Jhenya" from Mariupol, Ukraine. When he's not writing from his home office, Kyle loves to fish the eastern Sierras and hike the West's national parks. He and his wife, Suzanne, also have three biological daughters and make their home in San Diego, California.

Connect with Kyle

kyle@kyleduncan.co

kyleduncan.co

@kyle.duncan.7758

@kduncan

Esther Fedorkevich is a literary and entertainment agent and the founder of The Fedd Agency. With over eighty *New York Times* bestsellers on her list and twenty years in the industry, she is known for representing faith-based authors, athletes, influencers, politicians, and businesspeople to help them share their inspirational and hope-filled stories with the world. With the strong belief that everyone has a book in them, Esther is passionate about helping people realize the power of their message. Esther currently lives in Austin with her husband, Jimmy, and their two kids, Alexi Jane and Paul Gregory. To speak with Esther about representation, please email info@thefeddagency .com.

Connect with Esther

thefeddagency.com

- @TheFeddAgency
- @thefeddagency
- @thefeddagency
- @company/thefeddagency
- @thefeddagency